W9-AGB-156

Why "Good Kids" Turn into Deadly Terrorists

WHY "GOOD KIDS" TURN INTO DEADLY TERRORISTS

Deconstructing the Accused Boston Marathon Bombers and Others Like Them

Alice LoCicero

Foreword by Michael Lamport Commons

 PRAEGER

AN IMPRINT OF ABC-CLIO, LLC
Santa Barbara, California • Denver, Colorado • Oxford, England

Copyright 2014 by Alice LoCicero

All rights reserved. No part of this publication may be reproduced, stored in a retrieval system, or transmitted, in any form or by any means, electronic, mechanical, photocopying, recording, or otherwise, except for the inclusion of brief quotations in a review, without prior permission in writing from the publisher.

Library of Congress Cataloging-in-Publication Data

LoCicero, Alice, 1945–
  Why "good kids" turn into deadly terrorists : deconstructing the accused Boston Marathon bombers and others like them / Alice LoCicero ; foreword by Michael Lamport Commons.
    pages cm
  Includes index.
    ISBN 978-1-4408-3188-1 (hardback) — ISBN 978-1-4408-3189-8 (ebook)
  1. Terrorists—Psychology. 2. Suicide bombers—Psychology. 3. Youth and violence. 4. Terrorism. 5. Boston Marathon Bombing, Boston, Mass., 2013. I. Title.
    HV6431.L634 2014
    363.325'11—dc23   2014005733

ISBN: 978-1-4408-3188-1
EISBN: 978-1-4408-3189-8

18 17 16 15 14   1 2 3 4 5

This book is also available on the World Wide Web as an eBook.
Visit www.abc-clio.com for details.

Praeger
An Imprint of ABC-CLIO, LLC

ABC-CLIO, LLC
130 Cremona Drive, P.O. Box 1911
Santa Barbara, California 93116-1911

This book is printed on acid-free paper ∞

Manufactured in the United States of America

To all who have provided care for victims
of the Boston Marathon bombings

and

To all who work for social justice and human rights

Contents

Foreword

This book presents a very clear story that tells how some young people became terrorists and how the people around them, including thoughtful, well-intentioned, and open-minded people around the United States, do not understand how this can happen. This lack of understanding has a big impact on our policy toward terrorism and its prevention. Unless we develop a more complex view, we will pay a high price for fighting terrorism in very unsuccessful, economically expensive, and politically damaging ways. The value of this book is that it encourages a more nuanced and complex approach to understanding terrorist actions done by young people to the surprise of those who knew them.

The book starts out with a synopsis of what took place in the Boston bombing in 2013. It then goes on to report on many of the misguided commonsense theories of how the Tsarnaev brothers, Dzhokhar in particular, went from good, normal, American kids to dreaded jihadists. One thing that the book points out is that people in the United States, even in liberal and diverse Cambridge, Massachusetts, do not understand that many Americans (especially immigrants) often live in two or more cultures. They switch back and forth among languages and cultures. This is often called code switching.

From an evolutionary behavioral science perspective, terrorism can be considered as a conflict between two evolutionary forces: assortativeness and affiliativeness. Assortativeness is showing a preference for membership in a group whose members share a large number of characteristics.

Part of assortativeness is to defend one's own group and aggress against other groups that do not share those characteristics. Assortativeness might lead to the formation of actual and virtual terrorist groups in that individuals, even when living within a seemingly benign culture, may still feel a strong affiliation with a different group, while having shifting levels of affiliation with the relatively benign group around them. On the other hand, affiliativeness *promotes social cohesion* by being inclusive.

Instead of understanding this, the people around them see the two young men in overly simplistic ways. For example, they might posit that the only explanation they need is that the older brother influenced Dzhokhar. This simple-minded thinking along with other simplistic theories is dispelled in this book. For example, other naïve theories include the idea that the brothers' actions are explained fully by the idea that they did not have much to do, they lacked guidance when their parents left and went back to Dagestan, they were bored thrill-seekers, and most often that they were mentally ill. More troubling were the notions that they hated the United States all along and had hidden that from everyone. Or that mere exposure to online Islamic websites was enough to radicalize them, and/or that they were unthinking followers, directed by foreign or domestic terrorist groups. While many Americans wonder which of these factors was responsible, it is rare for people to recognize that there could be a combination of many factors. Unlike other current accounts of terrorism, this book develops and presents an integrative and multidimensional account that incorporates developmental, historical, and political factors.

It starts with the premise that terrorism is not just located in the terrorist but is an approach to conflicts around the world and throughout history. To understand why they did what they did, one must study the history of the places the terrorists come from, what the conflicts are, how people act in these conflicts. This can help one understand why terrorism might appear to be a good strategy to them. To understand the terrorists, one must consider what the person's experiences were, not just in their life directly but what they were exposed to indirectly, through reading, media, and accounts from others within the group they feel a part of. People may be traumatized by learning about and witnessing what has happened to "their people" even if they did not directly experience those events. There is a long chain of events that form the conflicts in which terrorists act. These are not limited just to contemporary issues and concerns. The chain of events is reflected in outcomes of many years, and even centuries, of actions, reactions, and interactions.

At the same time, the terrorists are changing as a result of their life circumstances and the impact of their travels, and they are also personally developing. Hence the book also uses developmental psychology using plain language to describe what is formally termed periods and stages of development. The use of stages and periods of development helps explain the constriction of the views that the young men develop. It shows that they are not able to integrate their multiple cultures and allegiances. It also shows how the lawlessness of the culture from which they came traumatizes them and makes it difficult for them to develop a more complex view. This is one of the major outcomes from living or being exposed to lawlessness for many people. It shows the extremely high cost in terms of the long-term success of these cultures of the use of extreme punishment by governments and also by their opponents. It also shows that the relatively low stage of political development is not just an attitude that can be shed by exposing people to more "enlightened" ways. That is, being in a relatively free, democratic culture is not an automatic cure for the cognitive and emotional costs of past trauma, although safety sets the stage for possible recovery. In the long run, political change in the home culture will help prevent trauma. This cannot be done suddenly; cultures change by stages, with many steps along the way.

The book includes an extensive discussion of the differences and similarities among terrorism, insurrection, gang activity, and solo mass shooters. It shows that terrorism is multilevel, with recruiters and their followers who commit the acts of terror having different interests and personal natures. The terrorists, including the recruiters, are using terrorism as an approach to asymmetry in resources. Terrorism, they hope, will even out the playing field. The gangs lack a political set of goals beyond the domination of a territory or activity. In common, gangs, insurrections, and terrorism may reflect the feeling that the weaker group is not being heard, and their interests and grievances are ignored by the governments and the society.

What if dissident groups, including terrorists, were given free and uncensored cable channel access? Or a place at a negotiating table? Would they feel that they needed to engage in terror to get people's attention? Our society fears their messages, but free speech seems to promote affiliation over the long run. A method that has large success in many countries is to bring the dissident factions into the governance structure, thereby giving them a real voice.

Most importantly, this book ends with hopeful evidence that humans have become, and continue to become, less violent over many years. This evidence provides hope that by considering multiple factors all at once, it is possible to develop solutions that actually address the sources of terrorism and, over time, to reduce and ultimately eliminate the need for such activity.

Michael Lamport Commons
Harvard Medical School
Cambridge, Massachusetts

Acknowledgments

First and foremost, I want to thank those who work tirelessly, every day, for genuine mutual understanding, education, and acceptance of differences, in families, communities, and organizations. You are providing a pathway to empathy and peace, and away from the "wrong perceptions" that, according to Zen Buddhist monk and teacher Thich Naht Hanh, are responsible for war and violence. Many who do this important work receive neither public appreciation nor compensation proportionate to the importance of the work, or to the time, energy, and care with which they do it.

Among those who work for mutual understanding, I want especially to thank those who work with refugees and asylum seekers, making the seemingly insurmountable challenges they face a bit easier to bear because they do not bear them alone.

Thanks, too, to those who work with adolescents and young adults who face life challenges, listening to them and helping them to shape good questions and good answers to life's dilemmas.

My family is lucky enough to have lived in the Boston area, and specifically in Cambridge, Massachusetts, and to have benefited from the dedication and competence of teachers and community leaders here. I want to thank them for their skills and care, even as I acknowledge, with them, that they, and we all, have much to learn.

Having benefited from discussions with so many accomplished colleagues about kids at risk of becoming terrorists, I felt prepared to help in understanding how good kids can perform heinous acts of violence. I am grateful for the wisdom of my colleagues, and their generosity in sharing it. Specifically, I thank my colleagues from the Society for Terrorism Research and from the Society for Research in Adult Development and its related organization, the European Society for Research in Adult Development, from whom I learned so much. Of course, the conclusions I drew and all I wrote here are my own, and I bear responsibility for any perspectives or statements or predictions that prove incorrect.

Immersing oneself in this painful material is a very lonely endeavor. Fortunately, good friends, family members, and colleagues were there to offer suggestions, find relevant articles I might have missed, inquire about my work, and sometimes about my feelings, since one cannot write about such material without being affected. They were also there to distract me, and to help me regain perspective. For that I shall be eternally grateful. Among them, but certainly not an exhaustive list, are Emily and James Crawford, Betty Kuhn, Patricia Thatcher, Mark Grossman, and Steve Seeche.

Various colleagues, including J. Martin Ramirez and James Pennebaker, kindly and generously shared their newest work, and I drew on it to supplement my thinking on various aspects of this work.

Michael Lamport Commons and Patti Miller have provided immeasurable help in understanding human development. We have shared discussions and created projects during travel over two decades and on three continents. With reference to this book, Michael generously provided help in the analysis of the implications of Dzhokhar Tsarnaev's writings. I also thank him for sharing his wisdom in the foreword to this book.

I am grateful for specific, timely, and expert help provided by my able and committed research assistant, editor, organizer, and all-around encourager, Emily Crawford.

I am fortunate to have had assistance from Pam Greenberg. I relied on her for suggestions, help with research, editing, clarification of ideas, and creation of the timeline.

For general support, encouragement, and interest that kept me going, I also want to thank my friends and colleagues at the Fuller 9 Writing Group, especially those who patiently heard my readings and kindly supported my work on this book: Shani Dowd, Orlando Lightfoot, and Jackie Vorpahl. I also want to thank my colleagues at Lesley University, Boston Medical Center, Community Legal Services and Counseling Center, the Cambridge Health Alliance Global Health and Human Rights Seminar, and Psychological Care Associates.

Thank you to my colleague Steve Noble, expert coach and advisor, for practical help and perspective, good sense, and encouragement at key points that helped me maintain focus on the mission.

Thanks to colleague Gil Noam, a great listener and Fresh Pond walking buddy, for providing wisdom, ideas, encouragement, and advice that was unfailingly accurate and helpful.

An earlier version of Chapter 4 was published in a literary journal called *The New Renaissance*. I benefited greatly from the meticulous editing by the founding editor of the journal, Louise Reynolds. Louise was not always able to be available, due to health challenges she faced. Patti Michaud stepped in for her, generously providing both editing and practical help at a moment's notice.

My colleague Samuel (Justin) Sinclair's positive influence provided the original inspiration for me to begin researching terrorism. While he did not work with me on this book, we have had so many discussions over the years and it would be hard to name a single aspect of my writing that did not have some resonance with our earlier shared work.

Kathryn Beaumont came through so many times, on short notice, and with skill and understanding, helping me work more effectively.

Several people, including Allison Gill and others, who had lived, studied, and worked in the Russian Federation, helped me gain information about Russia, and particularly the North Caucasus. I am indebted to them for their time and expertise.

Given the possibility that wrong perceptions might interfere with peoples' ability to understand that my intention is, as it has always been, to prevent kids from being recruited to lives immersed in violence, including terrorism, I anticipated the possibility that this book might be controversial. Others who also recognized that possibility chose not to be named. I understand their decision, and I will always appreciate the help they provided anonymously.

Finally, I want to thank Debbie Carvalko, who recognized the value of this project immediately and supported the complicated process from start to finish. Her vote of confidence was crucial and much appreciated. She consistently showed the most amazing mix of personal encouragement and professional competence.

To the extent this book is useful and helpful to those who are trying hard to puzzle out how a good kid could become involved in terrorism, I am indebted to all these helpful friends, colleagues, and family. But, of course, the final product is my personal responsibility alone.

Introduction

Obviously, tonight there are still many unanswered questions. Among them, why did young men who grew up and studied here, as part of our communities and our country, resort to such violence?
—Statement by President Barack Obama, April 19, 2013[1]

Hard as it is, incomplete as our understanding may be, and even though it brings us to the dimmest, ugliest, and most heinous corners of our society and the human community, we had better pursue the answers to the president's questions. We will never be 100 percent sure what was in the mind of Tamerlan Tsarnaev, killed in a police action a few days after the Boston Marathon bombing—we can only make guesses. But the guesses we make can, and should be, informed by the best science available. We will not have affirmation, for some time—if ever—of what was in the mind of Dzhokhar Tsarnaev, Tamerlan's younger brother, who was captured alive by police, at least not until his trial and maybe not even then. What we do have is a number of facts, a year and a half of Dzhokhar's tweets; some comments he apparently wrote while hiding in a boat in a resident's backyard in Watertown, Massachusetts, as he awaited either arrest or death, on April 19, 2013; a large amount of commentary by those who knew the Tsarnaevs, and a great deal of world news and social science research—on which to base our conclusions.

This book is about pain and trauma caused by two people, and it is also about hope for humanity inspired by tens or perhaps hundreds of thousands who have been inspired to help, in small and large ways, often at great cost to themselves.

Everywhere I turned while writing, I found evidence of people in pain, traumatized by loss, violence, injury, disappointment, confusion, and victimization: police who lost a brother and gained yet another reminder of the dangers of their work; family members and friends who will never again see, touch, hear, or hold their lost loved ones; injured victims, many now amputees, struggling to find ways to resume some aspects of the lives that were blown apart with pressure-cooker bombs on April 15; victims who suffered loss of sight or hearing; medical personnel and volunteers whose quick action to stop bleeding saved lives, but whose memories of that horrible day are not easily tamed; shocked and traumatized witnesses; innocent friends and acquaintances of the accused bombers who, wanting to help, found themselves interrogated by authorities desperate to protect society by diligently searching for any possible accomplices, anyone who might do further harm, hoping to apprehend them before it was too late; Watertown, Massachusetts, residents who were trapped inside their homes for many hours while the police looked for Dzhokhar Tsarnaev, believed to be armed and dangerous; a car-jacking victim, who spent about 30 or so minutes with a gun pointed at him by Tamerlan Tsarnaev, not knowing whether he would live to tell the story; runners who were turned back at mile 25, knowing their loved ones had been waiting at the finish line and not knowing if they were alive; employees of shops that were damaged, and those whose workplaces were simply too close for comfort, and who had trouble going back to work on April 16; American Muslims who have, for more than a decade, been treated as guilty by association with every terrorist action, even those found to be perpetrated by non-Muslims, and for whom the Boston Marathon bombings became another occasion leading to victimization, misunderstanding, and hatred directed at them, and law-abiding, patriotic Chechen Americans who, mortified by the actions of April 15, 2013, were soon reminded of how quickly the words "ethnic Chechen" stick to the word "terrorist." Every single day, in Boston, there are multiple reminders of individuals who still suffer: a runner trying out her new prosthesis; runners who cannot, yet, use a prosthesis; a child who lost her leg and lost her brother in one moment, showing amazing grace and resilience as she learns to run and dance; a police officer, or EMT, or surgeon, proud of their service, but traumatized as well; or a witness whose understanding of life was fundamentally changed in a fraction of second.

At the same time, I found evidence of the best of humanity. There are, every day, reminders of the generosity and care of Bostonians and others from around the world—moved by the courage of the victims—donating money, donating time, donating services, and doing what they can to help.

Months later, all over Boston, people are holding parties, dances, bake sales, and garage sales, with the goal of donating whatever they can to the fund for victims of the marathon attack, called the "One Fund,"[2] a reflection of a deep desire to help victims of the bombing. The One Fund dedicated to victims' needs has successfully eliminated confusion about where to donate. Bostonians do care a great deal, and want to help. And from this springs hope—a great deal of hope. The number of bombers: two. The number of people who have helped and continue to help: tens of thousands.

But besides the pain experienced by victims, and the outpouring of help, there is a kind of angst that cannot be easily seen, or understood. It is the concern of people in my home town of Cambridge, Massachusetts: moral pain and soul-searching, a sense of responsibility, of wondering how in the world this city—so proud of its schools, its track record of acceptance of immigrant students, its liberal politics—failed Tamerlan and Dzhokhar, and, in doing so, failed so many others whose lives have been permanently changed. Teachers, friends, neighbors, and other concerned citizens in Boston want to know how to make some meaning of this tragedy and hope to find clues that other towns do a better job of helping all youth find meaning in positive terms It is my deeply felt hope that this book will contribute to the discussion of how to help youth make positive meaning of their lives in ways that contribute to a peaceful future.

Despite all my experience, professional commitment, and scientific knowledge, I often struggled to continue writing this book, arguing with myself over whether I could afford to take the time to stop and weep for victims and for the thousands of young, misguided youth who are being led into actions that will effectively end their lives while ending the lives of others. Building a story out of the hundreds of puzzle pieces I found as I dug deeper into the events of April 15 and those that preceded them—despite help, advice, encouragement, and love from others—was, in the end, a lonely endeavor. Ironically, it was in those moments of loneliness when, I believe, I had the greatest insight into the good kids who were recruited to terrorism. They, it seems, were also alone in some fundamental way with their own attempts to create their life stories—the life stories I was trying to understand—out of disparate pieces of knowledge, including knowledge of the deep pain and suffering of members of their families and communities, past and present, and a deep longing to have a meaningful life. They had much to cry about, and were challenged to make meaning. As young men and women, misguided, perplexed, undoubtedly feeling alone with the most important decisions of their young lives, were vulnerable. It seems to me that in each case that vulnerability was taken advantage of by some recruiter whose self-serving actions led the youth seeking meaning to a terrible choice that ended the possibility of having a productive life or making a positive contribution to society.

For Dzhokhar, it seems, it was only a matter of time until he was no longer able to keep up appearances of being "chill" and "normal" and "American." At some point, it all became too much. The supports fell away, he had only a handful of people in whom he could confide, and all of them were on the side of recruitment to terrorism. He did not have the ability to resist being recruited and was thus swept into a kind of international groupthink about religion and politics, but, in the end, like all ethnic warfare, about land and riches. Carrying within himself the results of generations of trauma, he seems, from his tweets and from others' accounts, to have often been hungry, sleepless, broke, puzzled, high, and lonely. He no longer had the community of support and identification that could perhaps have seen him through or provided a viable alternative or helped him define his identity or decide where his loyalties should be, and that could have helped him find effective ways to work for change. Instead he got seduced, as so many young people do, into actions effective only in causing pain and confusion, not in causing change or insight. He was seduced into seeing the world in stark terms of good and evil, where he found it impossible to figure out which is which.

Regrettably, the Tsarnaevs are not the only young adults, thought by their friends and neighbors to be sweet, normal, and promising, who are alleged to have engaged in violence and terrorism in 2013. Nor is this the first decade, or even the first century, in which large-scale violence has been perpetrated by young people in all parts of the world. By now, one might think, we should have a good understanding of this phenomenon.

The Boston Marathon pressure-cooker bombs turned a happy and nonpolitical celebration into a hell, which, for a short period of time, bore an eerie resemblance to the reality of life for many in the small country of Chechnya (itself a "Small Corner of Hell"[3]), Colombia, Syria, Uganda, Somalia, South Sudan, or any of dozens of places in the world that were wracked with daily violence in 2013. Those who were at the finish line learned in an instant what life is like in a war zone, such as Chechnya was during its recent wars.

Dzhokhar became, it seems, convinced that the United States' wars in the Middle East are just one more Crusade against Muslims. And that bombing a joyous sporting event is justified as a response, just as bombing and violence were rampant and violence is stil carried on often with impunity in the Chechnya he identified with. In September 2013, the International Crisis Group report on the North Caucasus, including Chechnya and Dagestan, said:

Almost two decades of abusive behaviour by law enforcement personnel have eroded citizens' belief in the rule of law and pushed some victims into the Islamist insurgency, as earlier Crisis Group reporting has described. Impunity has embedded violence in security-service practices, even when investigating petty crimes. Human rights groups have extensively documented enforced disappearances, torture and summary executions, but victims lack effective domestic remedies. The last hope for redress for many is the European Court of Human Rights (ECtHR), where Russia has the largest docket of pending cases.[4]

It seems he, like so many youth in all parts of the world, became enamored of the false idea that he could, by destroying others' lives and his own life, make things better for other Muslims, and redress the wrongs they had suffered. It is sad that none of these young men and women will be able to put their passions to work in ways that might actually change the world for the better.

It seems, then, that to understand the origin of the Boston Marathon bombing—our day from hell—we cannot limit our inquiry to Cambridge, or Boston, or even to Chechnya. We must be willing to listen and talk with those who, in the 21st century, see the world in terms radically different from our own. This challenge arises for those of us who would like to prevent young men and women from sacrificing their lives to kill innocent civilians in a misguided logic that indicates that a violent lose-lose event will somehow help the people with whom they identify.

1

Shock and Disbelief: Friends and Neighbors React to the News about the Accused Brothers

Finally in the #bridge.

May 18, 2012

knowledge, strength, faith, money, love and success i'm hungry for it all

May 21, 2012

my niece is the cutest in the world

May 24, 2012

Idk why it's hard for many of you to accept that 9/11 was an inside job, I mean I guess fuck the facts y'all are some real #patriots #gethip

September 12, 2012

Cambridge got some real, genuinely good people but at the same time this city can be fake as fuck just like any other town

January 15, 2013

Cambridge remembers Dzhokhar Tsarnaev as the kind of person who could have written the first three of the tweets at the start of this chapter.

He was happy to be in town, and had big goals for his future. He was caring, kind, and able to appreciate others. He was a likeable guy who was like them and one of them; who had a home, a family, and a group of friends to hang out with; who was voted captain of the wrestling team at Cambridge Rindge and Latin High School where he fit in with other students in the diverse student body, including about 27 percent for whom English was not their first language;[1] who once told a teacher[2] that his family had come here to escape violence, and that he was glad they had ended up in Cambridge; and who was smart and popular and liked to party and smoke marijuana with his friends.

But in fact Dzhokhar wrote them all. Was the Dzhokhar they remember the real Dzhokhar? Was it an act? Surely those who knew him had missed something—but how could they miss something on this scale? This question, pressing as it is to those who knew Dzhokhar in Cambridge, should be urgent to all of us, for if we can understand what caused him to participate in placing bombs near the finish line of the Boston Marathon, killing a police officer, carjacking and holding the car's owner hostage, and engaging the police in a firefight when they tried to arrest him and his brother, we may have a glimmer of hope of preventing other young people in Western countries from deciding that the best meaning they can make of their lives is to sacrifice those lives for a cause—in this case Islam—protesting what seem to them to be very legitimate grievances.

For some weeks after the Tsarnaev brothers (Dzhokhar and Tamerlan) were accused of the Boston Marathon bombing,[3] shocked, horrified, and rather dazed friends, neighbors, teachers, and coaches of the brothers tried to combine two seemingly irreconcilable images: memories of the two mostly ordinary young men they knew, and reports of two evidently brutal, inhumane, destructive terrorists. Especially those who knew Dzhokhar, who seemed so well adjusted, wondered how could he be the same person? Many spoke to the press openly about this dilemma, only to find they had become public figures themselves, watched with some degree of suspicion. They began to worry they might be perceived as supporting or approving of these now officially accused terrorists. As a result, they stopped talking openly and publicly. A few continued to speak, anonymously, for a period of time.

In July 2013, *Rolling Stone*, an American music, politics, and popular culture magazine, released its August issue, with an attractive, evidently enhanced photo of Dzhokhar Tsarnaev on its cover. Quite an uproar followed. There was much criticism of this choice by those who saw it as raising his image to the level of a rock star—not a surprising comparison, since the magazine has often featured actual rock stars on its cover.

Indeed, the cover received considerably more media attention than the actual article about Tsarnaev featured inside the magazine. The issue was boycotted by some stores and harshly criticized; nevertheless, it sold twice the usual number of copies. This might, of course, be simply a reflection of the saying: "all publicity is good publicity." It may also be an expression of the complex reactions by many who had intensely mixed feelings about the accused bombers. On the one hand, many felt deeply puzzled and driven to try to understand how these young men, who were connected to their local communities, who had friends, neighbors, teachers, and coaches who cared for them, could decide to perpetrate heinous acts toward innocent people. On the other hand, others felt that it was somehow morally wrong to give cover-story attention to someone who could, in a seemingly matter-of-fact manner, kill, maim, and terrorize innocent people, some from the communities he lived in; victims who were athletes or who came out to celebrate the successes of athletes who had completed a 26.2-mile run. Indeed, one of the law enforcement officers who was at the scene when Dzhokhar surrendered and emerged from a boat in a resident's backyard in Watertown, Massachusetts, on April 19, 2013, made public some photos of a bloodied and helpless Dzhokhar, evidently in an attempt to right the wrong impression he believed the public might get from the *Rolling Stone* cover.

The much less-discussed actual *Rolling Stone* article by Janet Reitman[4] reflects the shock experienced by Dzhokhar's peers in particular, many of whom spoke only anonymously out of fear that they might be seen as an affiliate of a terrorist—their friend's new identity. Reading their comments—such as references to him as "sweet," "a good kid," "super-chill," and "just a normal American kid"[5]—together with the comments of others who spoke to the press in the aftermath of the bombing, one can hardly miss the hallmark American blissful melting-pot belief that immigrants soon become assimilated. And in the assimilation process, all the pain and trauma experienced by immigrants in the country of origin is washed away.

This unfortunate belief is likely perceived by many as reflecting cluelessness on the part of fortunate Americans who have not personally experienced violence or chaos. It seems likely that such a perception would lead to some mix of envy and resentment. On the one hand, an immigrant such as Dzhokhar might think that it would be nice to be privileged enough to not have a legacy of violence. On the other hand, some Americans' failure to acknowledge others' painful pasts may seem like flaunting the unearned right to be ignorant and blissful. While the privileged American may justify not mentioning the immigrant's past as wanting the immigrant to feel included, the immigrant may well see it as a reflection of the American's lack of care, lack of knowledge, and lack of empathy. In the case of an immigrant like Dzhokhar, whose identity as a Muslim puts him at risk of being misunderstood, profiled, stereotyped, and hated, it might seem even bizarre and shocking that his friends were not paying attention to this aspect of his life. In this respect, Cambridge, progressive as it may be, is no more attuned than much of America. It is accepting of immigrants, including refugees, but by its very progressiveness, it may lead the immigrants in its midst to feel that that acceptance is conditional on feeling happy to be openly accepted and on agreeing with the self-congratulatory sense of those doing the accepting, at least outwardly. It seems that this bargain worked for Dzhokhar for a while, but in the end, it left him alone with his painful dilemma—a dilemma that none of his peers or the adults in his life were aware of.

Many Americans seem to have a tendency to see refugees and those granted asylum and a path to citizenship as being lucky and as having an obligation to assimilate. A hint of this is found in the reinvented spelling and pronunciation of Dzhokhar's name, to "Jahar," which was easier for his American friends and teachers to pronounce. Dzhokhar is an important name in Chechnya—perhaps even a controversial one. Dzhokhar Dudayev, voted president of Chechnya in 1991 by 85 percent of voters, declared Chechnya an independent republic. Dzhokhar's father, Anzor, is said to have had a strongly positive attitude toward Dudayev. None of that was taken into account, however, by those Americans who wanted to refer to him in a way that was easier for them. Minor, perhaps, but also perhaps symbolic of the expectation that Dzhokhar bend to the needs of the Americans to become a bit more like an American, rather than the Americans making the effort to learn the spelling and pronunciation of his name. Indeed many Americans tend to think it is a compliment to say, of an immigrant, that you would never know he or she was not born here, without thinking about why that should be a good thing. Perhaps that is not the fault of third- and fourth-generation Americans, since earlier generations—in many cases their grandparents or great grandparents—tended to want to Americanize as rapidly as possible. Many of those great grandparents and grandparents seemed to be ashamed of their ethnic, immigrant past, and to be eager for their children to be as American as apple pie. There is a classic line in *Hester Street*, a film about early 20th-century immigration. In it, an immigrant father is gushing with pride over his young son, saying the son looks "just like a Yankee!"[6] Although life was very hard for immigrants then—many lived and worked with ever-present danger—there was, inarguably, an upward trend for each generation, providing a guarantee that if one worked hard and saved carefully, one's children would have a better life. We underestimate the importance of this upward mobility—and its absence in contemporary American society—at our peril.

HOW DID CAMBRIDGE FAIL DZHOKHAR?

Dzhokhar's wrestling coach, Peter Payack, is quoted by Reitman:[7] "'I felt like a bullet went through my heart,' the coach recalls. 'To think that a kid we mentored and loved like a son could have been responsible for all this death. It was beyond shocking. It was like an alternative reality.'"

Peers, teachers, neighbors, friends, and family members wonder how they could have missed that Dzhokhar was, deep down, a monster who would soon kill, maim, and terrify his city and country; who would systematically download instructions and construct bombs designed to harm people, and place one of them among a crowd of innocent civilians. Even now, they ponder how they missed the real "Jahar." But what if they didn't? What if the Jahar they saw was the real deal? Chill, Americanized, smart, helpful, sweet? One of them. That was then. What if the change occurred after he left high school? After his family fell apart. After his father became sick and moved thousands of miles away, and his family became poor, and he racked up a huge amount of debt. He had to make a decision. And what if it was a heartrending decision about what was good and what was evil?

> In the United States, group-defined identities play a role in adolescent development, although the groups doing the defining include groups of choice, as well as groups into which one was born. Harvard Professor and Psychologist Robert Kegan discussed this issue of identity formation in youth, and using mostly examples from individually oriented cultures still concluded that youth almost invariably define "self" in terms of the social institutions to which they belong. Social groups essentially become the framework used for understanding the basic identity question: Who am I? Answers include: I am an athlete on the baseball team, a musician in the band, an academic competing on the math team, the president of the Civics Club. (Not, note, I am the son of so and so, a member of this ethnic group, a resident of this town.) The social group is what leads to a sense of identity-even if, in the United States, the social group is a chosen group, joined more or less voluntarily. Still, without it, confusion and even crisis result.[8]

Dzhokhar very likely did identify with his American peer group, while it was intact, while it had support and structure from high school, and sports, and gatherings and parties. He was part of that group. It was when the group's influence began to fall away, as it does after graduation, that the group could no longer afford Dzhokhar a sense of identity, and he was left to define himself, open to other influences, and, sadly, unprepared for the literally life and death decisions that were ahead of him.

It seems likely that the first three tweets listed at the start of the chapter reflected a time when Dzhokhar was still accessible, still open to a variety of options about where his life would go: happy to be back in town, able to enjoy his baby niece. By the fourth tweet, it seems clear to me, and to others who have studied his tweets (Norman and Pennebaker, 2013), that he had chosen to look at things a different way. To believe that he had to depart from the familiar environment of his youth, which he now saw as "fake as fuck," and choose to ally with his brother, and with other young men who saw violence as justified, and even required, to avenge the lives of Muslims killed by Christians, and then by Christian nations, over the past thousand or so years. This entire transition has evidently happened to numerous Muslim youth in Western countries, and we have surely not seen the end of it. It is therefore necessary for Cambridge and other cities to think hard about what can be done to prepare young men and women for these young-adult transitions and the likelihood that some adult who will benefit—at the very least in reputation—by recruiting them will come along and present a compelling argument for violence. These recruiters, unlike the American peers and adults in the lives of Dzhokhar and others like him, know their history very well, and know how to use that history to market terrorism and persuade otherwise good kids to sign up.

The change was subtle enough, and Dzhokhar secretive enough, that his friends, neighbors, teachers, and fellow students only saw in retrospect the subtle signs of a troubled transition. And they were more or less dragged, kicking and screaming, into seeing that he was one of the bombers who caused death, destruction, pain, and chaos. They were in shock and disbelief, as much as if a disaster of monstrous proportions had overcome the city. In fact, it could be argued, it had.

Perhaps Cambridge did not so much fail Dzhokhar while he was there, in school, a kid, as it failed to prepare him for the challenges that lay ahead, for the toughest choices he would face in his young life. Challenges like how to reconcile the multiple identities he held, as a young Muslin man in a predominantly Christian culture, as an ethnic Chechen in America, as an invisible minority, as an immigrant, as a member of a poor family in an affluent city, as a young man who liked marijuana even though his religion forbade it. And perhaps most poignantly, as a young man in a family that was divided between those who favored a devout, unyielding, fundamentalist form of Islam and those who identified with an Islam that was more relaxed, that accommodated local customs and practices, that defined a person's core values but not his or her every action and thought.

While Dzhokhar was a kid, his peers and teachers and neighbors enjoyed the convenient fiction that he was finding it easy to assimilate—indeed perhaps was already completely assimilated. Only a few seemed to vaguely acknowledge that he had a life burdened by history. One of his teachers, for example, says that Dzhokhar identified himself as Chechen. When asked how he had managed to cope, Dzhokhar reportedly said that the difficulties there were the reason his family had come to the United States, and noted how lucky it was that they had come to Cambridge. The teacher accepted that response at face value.[9] Later, that teacher, also taken in by Dzhokhar's evidently studied, and marijuana-aided, exterior as a well-adjusted, good kid, told reporters that it was impossible that Dzhokhar could be the bomber.

Indeed, some of Dzhokhar's classmates, friends, family members, and admirers still insist that he is innocent, was framed, or was at least coerced into blowing up the pressure-cooker bombs. They showed up at his June hearing, turning it into something of a political rally. And they have an active website, www.freejahar.net, on which they present what they seem to think passes for evidence that he was not the actual bomber. This evidence ranges from the interesting and intriguing, such as the following quotes found on the website:

> It is a FACT that the backpack pictured at Dzhokhar's feet outside of Forum restaurant (the backpack said to have contained one of the bombs), does not match the backpack that Dzhokhar arrived with. It is also a FACT that the backpack at his feet also does not match pictures of the exploded backpack.

To the seemingly irrelevant, whether accurate or not, such as:

> It is a FACT that the exploded backpack is very similar to those purchased by the Department of Homeland Security for use by Navy Seals.

While the website accurately reports that the person initially arrested for bombing the Atlanta Olympics was later determined to be innocent, it fails to take account of the myriad of photo and video evidence, the first-person accounts, or Dzhokhar's tweets, or what he wrote in the boat while awaiting death or discovery on April 19, 2013.

The July *Rolling Stone* article by Reitman provides a solid account of the complicated, concerned thoughts and feelings of several of Dzhokhar's friends in the months following the bombing, for example, comments like "this shakes me to my core."[10] Perhaps equally telling, if not more so, are the comments and tweets of his friends and family within hours and days after the bombing. Many of them could not coordinate, much less integrate, in their minds, the Dzhokhar they knew with the Dzhokhar who was on the run from police, discovered bloody and perhaps hopeless in a boat in a backyard in Watertown, Massachusetts.

A few months out, it is hard to get anyone to talk about Dzhokhar. It seems dangerous to do so, since no one wants to be associated with an accused terrorist, have the FBI very interested in them, or lose their privacy. The young man whom people identified as chill and sweet, and as helping anyone who needed help, is now, in his absence, a pariah. In choosing the path he chose, he had to see the bad in America, and by extension, in his friends and neighbors and they had to see the bad in him.

A May 2013 *Washington Post-ABC News* poll found that 70 percent of Americans would favor the death penalty for Dzhokhar Tsarnaev if he is found guilty.[11] By contrast, in September 2013, just four months later, a *Boston Globe* poll found that only 33 percent of Bostonians would favor the death penalty for Dzhokhar if he is found guilty.[12] Perhaps this reflects a more general difference in attitudes toward the death penalty. There is no capital punishment under Massachusetts law, and no executions have occurred in Massachusetts since 1947. Nationally, support for the death penalty in general is waning, with a recent Gallup poll showing that 60 percent of Americans now favor this form of punishment for convicted murderers, the lowest percentage since the 1970s.[13]

GOING BEYOND SOUND BITES AND COMMON-SENSE THEORIES

In my travels around the greater Boston area, and in listening to mass media, I have heard many common-sense theories of how the Tsarnaev brothers, Dzhokhar in particular, went from good, normal, American kids to dreaded jihadists, seemingly right before the eyes of their friends and acquaintances, neighbors, teachers, and family members. The top theory seems to be that Dzhokhar was influenced, persuaded, or even brainwashed by his older brother. Other theories include the idea that the brothers had too much time on their hands and/or too little guidance once their parents left; that they were thrill-seekers who were just bored with their humdrum lives; that they were mentally ill; that they had been haters all along but had hidden it; that they were forced into terrorism; that they were seduced and radicalized by online Islamic websites; that they were encouraged and/or supported by foreign or domestic terrorist groups; that they were tricked into it by others, possibly by the Russian government trying to "prove" that those of Chechen ethnicity are untrustworthy terrorists; that they were tricked into it by the U.S. government; or that they actually did not do it at all. Not only the website but also numerous peers, his parents, and some other members of the Chechen American community evidently continue to doubt that Dzhokhar and Tamerlan were fully responsible for the bombing, in spite of the comments written by Dzhokhar while in the boat in Watertown.

But the decision and transition from fully participating in one's community, accepting the role of a normal, good kid, to participating in a deadly terrorist act does not come quickly, based on one simple motive or decision point. As Moghaddam[14] reminds us, there are several steps in the transition, each one making the next one easier and more likely. Beyond Moghaddam's description of the process, however, we must consider that a long history of events, many of them having happened long before the Tsarnaev brothers were born and far away from Boston, is likely to have influenced the life of the family of the Tsarnaev brothers. These events, taking place over centuries and across continents, create a history that we must understand if we are to make sense of the events of April 15, 2013, in Boston, Massachusetts.

UNDERSTANDING HOW A GOOD KID BECAME AN ACCUSED TERRORIST VERSUS CONDONING THE ACTIONS

Ever since the terrible attacks on the United States on September 11, 2001, Americans have been engaged in many levels of conversation about how to respond to terrorists. At a very simplistic level, at least four approaches are evident. In the first approach, any attention other than punishment or assassination is equated with sympathetic approval, and those wanting to understand terrorists are excoriated as terrorism sympathizers, unpatriotic, and likely to encourage more terrorism by rewarding terrorist acts with attention. This approach tends to condemn even normal levels of curiosity, and is suspicious even of the scientific study of terrorism.[15] The second approach, equally simplistic, is the belief that terrorists are somewhat heroic actors, martyrs reacting with self-sacrifice in order to stop legitimate grievances, unfairness, and violations of human rights. In this approach, the actions of terrorists are thought to be motivated solely by the hope of bringing those violations to our attention. This approach assumes that righting these wrongs will end terrorism. Indeed, some go so far as to wonder why, given the large number of identifiable grievances in the United States and around the world, more people do not engage in terrorist actions. In the third simplistic approach, terrorists are assumed to be simply crazy or insane, and therefore no attempt to use reason to understand them is likely to be effective. The logical conclusion of the third view is that perhaps terrorists should not be assassinated but, rather, incarcerated permanently.[16] The fourth approach is that terrorists are weak individuals easily brainwashed by others who use them as fodder in their own struggles for power and fame.

While there may be, in any given instance of terrorism, some truth to any or all of these simple, common-sense approaches to understanding the acts committed, none of them tells the whole story, and none of them will get us very far in preventing future terrorism. It is likely true that the outbreak of terrorist activities beginning in the last quarter of the 20th century, like past outbreaks, will end for some reasons we cannot now predict, if we wait long enough.[17] Terrorist groups go out of business for a variety of reasons, including success (exemplified by the African National Congress) and infighting (exemplified by the Japanese organization Aum Shinrikyo).[18] And terrorism outbreaks end for reasons not always clear, such as the end of the anarchy movement in the early 20th century. But in the meantime, many more people will be killed and maimed, and, perhaps more importantly, our rights will be even more compromised. Our civil society will become less tolerant, less democratic, less free, subject to even more incursions on individual rights and individual privacy, more hated by those outside the country, and at the end of the day, still at risk. We cannot afford to wait for terrorism to die a natural death, as it has following past outbreaks. We must address the root causes of this outbreak of terrorism, and in the process learn how to reduce and/or prevent further attacks.

As has been stated by terrorism experts for some time, the best answers to the questions about terrorism are both nuanced and complex. Understanding should not be equated with approving of terrorists, nor should it be understood as denying the horrible impact of their actions. Rather, it should be understood as an attempt to prevent terrorism by dispelling the myths told to potential recruits, and also by ending the conditions that lead to its use.

After World War II, efforts to understand the Nazi movement became a major—if not the only—focus of study by American social scientists. They felt that in order to prevent another catastrophic blow to our civilization, we needed to understand what had happened, why, and how the Nazis had received enough support and power to threaten civilization as we knew it. Topics like authoritarianism, communism, fascism, and obedience continue to be represented in psychological research.

And in Nuremberg, Germany, the victorious Allies—Russia, France, the United Kingdom, and the United States—took deliberate, rational, cautious steps to weigh the evidence against some of the world's most heinous criminals. In the words of Supreme Court Justice Robert Jackson, in November 1945, at the opening of the Nuremberg trials:

> That four great nations, flushed with victory and stung with injury stay the hand of vengeance and voluntarily submit their captive enemies to the judgment of the law is one of the most significant tributes that Power has ever paid to Reason.[19]

Understanding terrorists is another way to make power take a backseat to reason. If we can use our best reasoning abilities to understand what happened to accused bombers Dzhokhar and Tamerlan Tsarnaev, we will have come a long way toward finding ways to prevent or at least reduce future terrorism. We will have used reason to fight violence.

HISTORY: THE FIFTH DIMENSION

When studying terrorism and terrorists from a social science perspective, one must consider biological, psychological, sociocultural, and political factors. But there is another dimension that is often missed: the historical dimension. Terrorist actions reflect far more than contemporary issues and concerns. They reflect, in addition, the outcome of many years, and even centuries, of actions, reactions, and interactions. The roots of the 26-year civil war in Sri Lanka were laid down over centuries of Portuguese, Dutch, and British occupation. The roots of the Chechen wars in the 1990s include events in the 18th century. And likewise, the root causes of events of April 15, 2013, include situations that took place over a thousand years earlier.

These roots include early intense conflict between Muslims and Christians that was never fully resolved but simmered over centuries. They also include the history of Chechnya in relation to Russia, a history that led to the Tsarnaev brothers' grandfather being expelled from Chechnya and their father being persecuted because he was an ethnic Chechen.

These roots likely also include the cultural concept of what it is to be a strong person, and in particular a strong man, in Chechnya. They also include the decisive break between Sunni and Shia Muslims, the conflict among Christians, Jews, and Muslims over Jerusalem and the Holy Land, and the historic events of 1948 that gave persecuted Jews a homeland—Israel. These same events were experienced by Palestinians as *Nabka,* or catastrophe.

History, despite the complaints of many students, is alive and well in the minds and hearts of all of us, whether we are aware of it or not.

TIMELINE LEADING TO THE BOSTON MARATHON BOMBINGS

We ignore history at our peril. But knowing history alone will not help us better understand why the Boston Marathon bombings took place. Rather, we must integrate the personal and family history with the social and political historical events that influenced the accused bombers. We offer, next, an annotated timeline—one that should begin to explain, to Cambridge citizens and others, some of the many factors that led to the bombing at the Boston Marathon, and what the people of Cambridge missed that might have helped them assist the Tsarnaev brothers to have a better chance at fulfilling their best possible future, rather than having their future now determined by events over which well-meaning people of Cambridge ultimately had no control.

Timeline

The timeline may allow readers to come to a wide range of theories and hunches about what happened, perhaps giving Cambridge residents and those who knew Dzhokhar a few things to think about. Following the timeline, Chapter 2 discusses some common elements in 21st-century terrorism, and Chapter 3 applies social science principles to the data found in the first two chapters in order to establish a working hypothesis of why Dzhokhar, a good kid with a potentially promising mainstream future, chose to make a political statement that cost him that future, just as surely as that political statement cost his brother his life. The timeline that follows includes many threads of events that may have played a part in the eventual decision, allegedly made by Dzhokhar Tsarnaev, to bomb the Boston Marathon. Here is a list of those threads:

1. Events from Dzhokhar's life and that of his family.
2. Events in the history of Chechnya.
3. Events in the life of Hassan Abdi Dhuhulow, another good kid who evidently became a terrorist. Dhuhulow was an immigrant to Norway from Somalia. He is accused of being one of the terrorists who attacked the Westgate Mall in Nairobi in September 2013.
4. Events that might be interpreted as part of the conflict between Islam and Christianity.
5. Recent terrorist attacks, planned or executed, against the United States and that affected the United States.

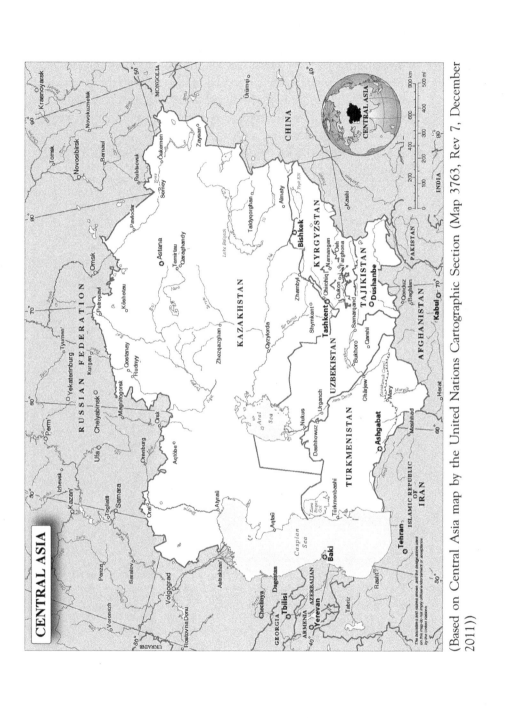

(Based on Central Asia map by the United Nations Cartographic Section (Map 3763, Rev 7, December 2011))

TIMELINE

1095 Pope Urban launches the first of the Crusades, urging European Christians to assist Greece in regaining Palestine from Muslim Seljug Turks. A series of Crusades follow, extending into the 17th century.[1]

1336–1405 Lifespan of Tamerlane (Timur the Lame), a successful Mongol warrior. Although his story is not well known in the west, he was a celebrated warrior, and even the subject of an opera by Handel.[2]

1785 Chechens make the first attempt to resist Russian encroachment on their land.[3]

1859 Chechnya is annexed to Russia following a bloody war in which Russia takes much of the Caucasus.[4]

1885 Thirty-nine thousand Chechens are exiled to Turkey by Tsarist authorities.[5]

Late 1800s Early stages of contemporary ongoing Middle East conflict over homeland for people of different faiths and cultures.[6]

1933 Zaindy, father of Anzor Tsarnaev, is born in Chechnya.[7]

1944 Zaindy and his family are deported from Chechnya to Tokmok, Kyrgyztan, during a massive forced migration under Stalin. Hundreds of thousands of Chechens are killed or die along the way. The Tsarnaevs work as farmers and sheepherders in a largely urban area.[8]

1948 Declaration of the state of Israel.[9]

1957 Chechens are allowed to return to Chechnya, causing some difficulties with others who have moved there between 1944 and 1957.[10]

ca. 1964 Anzor Tsarnaev is born.[11] Anzor is one of 10 siblings, several of whom become lawyers.[12]

1978 Mosques are allowed to reopen in Chechnya.[13]

ca. 1984 Anzor meets his wife, Zubeidat, in Elista, the provincial capital of the Kalmykia region, where they were both students. Zubeidat, an ethnic Avar (a group that is mostly Muslim), came from Dagestan.[14]

October 20, 1986	Anzor and Zubeidat marry in Kalmykia.[15]
October 21, 1986	Tamerlan Tsarnaev is born.[16]
1988	Anzor's father, Zaindy, is killed in an accidental explosion of munitions in Tokmok, Kyrgyztan (now Kyrgyz Republic).[17]
1990–91	First Gulf War. Iraq invades Kuwait and attempts to take it over. U.S. Congress authorizes the use of force to drive Iraq out of Kuwait. A brief war begins in January 1991 and ends in March 1991, taking place both in the air and on the ground.
Fall 1991	Dzhokhar Dudayev, the new president of Chechnya, declares Chechen sovereignty. A period of internal conflict within Chechnya begins.[18]
December 1991	The Soviet Union is dissolved.
1992	The Tsarnaevs briefly return to Chechnya and are apparently dissuaded by conditions there. By some accounts they fled when the war began, and were at grave risk during the flight, returning to Kyrgyztan with bullet holes in their car.[19] They move back to Kyrgyztan where their other children, Ailina, Bella, and Dzhokhar, are born. Anzor gets a job as an investigator in a prosecutor's office in Bishkek.[20]
July 22, 1993	Dzhokhar Tsarnaev is born.[21]
1994–96	The First Chechen War begins when Russian president Boris Yeltsin orders the Russian Army to occupy Chechnya and ends the Dudayev government. The fighting continues for nearly two years.[22]
April 19, 1995	Domestic terrorists Timothy McVeigh and Terry Nichols, veterans who had met in basic training, attack the Murrah Federal Building in Oklahoma City as a protest to the FBI's handling of two standoffs. It seems that McVeigh thought that the attack might ultimately save lives by enlightening others to the problems he perceived.
1995	Human Rights Watch reports both Chechen and Russian fighters violating human rights.[23] Life for ordinary Chechens is very difficult.[24]

1999	Family of Hassan Abdi Dhuhulow emigrates from Somalia to Norway.[25] Dhuhulow's story contains parallels to that of the Tsarnaevs.
August 1999	The War of Dagestan begins when the Chechnyan-based Islamic International Brigade invades Dagestan in support of separatists there. This sparks the Second Chechnyan War; Russia and its supporters invade Chechnya and face separatists in open combat for several months. Russia eventually gains control over Chechnya, but resistance fighters persist for several years.[26]
1999	Anzor is fired from his job shortly after war breaks out in Chechnya.[27] He is sent to jail and subjected to beatings.[28] Tamerlan, 14, is also subject to beatings by local police.[29]
1999	The Tsarnaev family moves briefly to Chechnya. They flee during the Russian invasion.[30]
2001	The Tsarnaev family moves to Machachkala, capital of Dagestan. This move evidently follows the persecution of Anzor, either by the authorities in Kyrgyztan, or by members of a Russian mob. One account indicates that the family's German Shepherd was decapitated by mob members.[31] Dzhokhar spends not even a full year in the school.[32]
September 11, 2001	Major terrorist attack in the United States, attributed to Al Qaeda, a group that is motivated by objections to Western lifestyle, to collaboration between the United States and Saudi Arabia, and to fear that the West meant to obliterate Islam. This event leads to a massive movement in the United States toward patriotism and increased suspicion of foreign-born individuals, especially Arabs and Muslims.
September 15, 2001	President George W. Bush uses the term "crusade" in discussing the "war on terrorism" launched following the September 11 attacks. Many European leaders are alarmed at the use of this term. The White House issues an apology.[33]

October 2001   The United States launches first attacks in long war in Afghanistan; this is considered to be a response to September 11 attacks.

December 22, 2001   Attempted, but failed, terrorist action by Richard Reid, the so-called shoe bomber. Reid is claimed to be an Al Qaeda operative, but this is generally doubted.

April 2002   Anzor, Zubeidat, and Dzhokhar come to the United States on a 90-day tourist visa, founding the company Credit Collections Bureau. Anzor applies for asylum in the United States, citing threats; Tamerlan and his sisters stay with an uncle in Kazakhstan. Once settled, Anzor begins working on cars.[34] Dzhokhar is enrolled at Cambridgeport School, skipping one grade after quickly catching up to age-mates despite initially limited English skills.[35] Anzor and Zubeidat were well educated and had professional degrees, and arrived with hope and high energy. They are reported to have received government assistance with housing and a living allowance.[36]

2003–2005   Anzor and Zubeidat receive psychiatric help from Dr. Alexander Niss, a psychiatric resident at St. Elizabeth's Hospital, Brighton, Massachusetts. Anzor is evidently suffering due to trauma prior to immigration to the United States.[37]

March 2003   The United States invades Iraq, on the premise of a connection between Iraq and the September 11, 2001, attacks.

July 2003   Tamerlan is in Turkey in July on a Kyrgyzstani passport.[38]

July 19, 2003   Tamerlan and his two sisters arrive in the United States, at JFK airport.[39]

2003   One of Dzhokhar's report cards describes him as having "a heart of gold."[40]

2004   Tamerlan enrolls at Cambridge Rindge and Latin School (CRLS) in its ESL Program[41] and develops an interest in boxing during his sophomore year.[42] He speaks with a thick Russian accent.[43]

2003–4 and 2008–10	Tamerlan is registered to fight with USA Boxing, the organization that oversees amateur boxing in the United States. He delivers pizza and holds other part-time jobs while boxing.[44] Early stories about his boxing talk about his style of keeping hands at his sides (not protecting his face) and refusing to use protective gear.[45] Other stories exist about him playing classical music on a piano during registration for a tournament.[46]
January 2004	In an interview with *The Lowell Sun* newspaper, Tamerlan says, "I like the USA . . . America has a lot of jobs. That's something Russia doesn't have. You have a chance to make money here if you are willing to work." He also tells the newspaper that he studied music at a school in Russia and played the piano and violin.[47] Tamerlan is well liked and is reportedly seen as good-natured, both at school and in youth boxing circles.[48]
ca. 2004	Family socialized with other Chechnyan families in Boston area.[49]
2004	Chechen militants lead a siege on a school in Beslan; more than 330 people, mostly children, are killed.[50]
2005	Anzor's brother Ruslan visits from Maryland and talks to Tamerlan about his future. Tamerlan plans to study engineering, then get a law degree.
2005–7	Dzhokhar transfers to the Community Charter School of Cambridge. He is one of the few white kids in a primarily African American school that stresses discipline.[51]
2006	Tamerlan applies to UMass Boston for fall 2006, but is rejected.[52] He attends Bunker Hill Community College during the fall 2006, spring 2007, and fall 2008 semesters.[53]
March 2007	The Tsarnaevs become permanent residents of the United States.[54]
2007	Tamerlan confronts the boyfriend of his sister Bella. Their father had not approved of her being seen with him. Tamerlan punches him in the face, reportedly because he was not Muslim.[55]

ca. 2008	Tamerlan reportedly tells others he has been hearing voices and that this is troubling to him.[56]
2008	Tamerlan "got involved in religion," according to his mother.[57] According to other reports, his mother encouraged him to turn to religion out of concern for his drinking, smoking, and womanizing.[58]
2008	Tamerlan becomes devout Muslim and begins to attend the Islamic Society of Boston mosque in Cambridge.[59] His girlfriend, Katherine Russell, begins wearing a hijab.[60]
Summer 2008	Tamerlan does well working with elderly clients in a Newton care organization.[61]
Late 2008	Ruslan Tsarni, uncle of Dzhokhar and Tamerlan, visits family from Maryland. Reportedly, he was very unhappy to see the family had become devout, above his brother Anzor's strenuous objections. He reportedly was especially unhappy with Zubeidat, and became alienated from the family.[62]
2009	Hassan Abdi Dhuhulow spends three months in Somalia and returns to Norway. Norwegian law enforcement authorities attempt to dissuade him from returning to Somalia, concerned he may be radicalized.[63]
2009	Katherine converts to Islam and takes the name Karima.[64]
2009	Anzor's health begins to deteriorate.[65]
2009	Tamerlan talks about two people living inside him. He meets "Misha," a thirty-something Armenian convert to Islam at a Boston-area mosque.[66]
April 2009	Tamerlan is photographed training at Wai Kru Mixed Martial Arts in Boston for a university magazine story. He describes himself as a native of Chechnya and says, "I don't have one American friend. I don't understand them."[67] Tamerlan tells his uncle he "is not concerned about work or studies because God has a plan for [him]."[68]
May 4, 2009	Tamerlan competes in the Golden Gloves National Tournament of Champions in Salt Lake City in the 201-pound division, having qualified

by winning the New England Golden Gloves Championship. He arrives wearing black leather pants, a white silk scarf, and mirrored sunglasses. He knocks down Lamar Fenner of Chicago with a punch that requires an eight-count from the referee, and seems to be ahead for the rest of the match. Bob Russo, then the coach of the New England team, says: "We thought he won. The crowd thought he won. But he didn't."[69]

July 28, 2009   Tamerlan is arrested, accused of domestic abuse and battery according to police records.[70]

Summer 2009   Anzor is severely injured following a dispute in a restaurant, where Anzor is accused of bumping into a guest's chair and refuses to apologize. His injuries were serious and warranted a one-week stay in a hospital, with headaches continuing for one year afterward.[71]

August 2009   The Tsarnaev family begins receiving public assistance benefits (food stamps and cash), partly because of Anzor's poor health. They had previously been off benefits for five years.[72]

December 25, 2009   Umar Farouk Abdulmutallab, known as the Underwear Bomber, attempts to blow up a flight from Amsterdam to Detroit. It is understood that he had support from Al Qaeda in the Arabian Peninsula. His attempt is foiled by a passenger.

2010   Reports indicate increased numbers of young men in Dagestan attacking police. This pattern of unrest has continued for over 10 years.[73]

2007–11   Dzhokhar attends CRLS. In his sophomore year he joins the wrestling team, and is elected captain two years in a row. He thrives on the team, perhaps in part due to the closeness and support it provides. Also during this time period, the Tsarnaev sisters move to New Jersey.

February 10, 2010   Tamerlan is awarded the Rocky Marciano Trophy, an honor given to the heavyweight champion of Massachusetts.[74]

2010   A rule change means that noncitizens are barred from competing nationally in boxing.[75]

March 2010   Hassan Abdi Dhuhulow departs Norway for
                  Somalia, despite efforts by the Norwegian Secu-
                  rity Service, PST.[76]

March 29, 2010   Two female Chechen suicide bombers kill more
                  than 40 people in the Moscow subway.

June 21, 2010   Tamerlan marries Karima (formerly Katherine)
                  Russell, a woman from a fairly wealthy family
                  in Rhode Island. According to *The New York
                  Times* the wedding took place in a Dorchester
                  mosque.[77] Other references say that they were
                  married in Cambridge by a city clerk. Neighbors
                  note a change in his appearance. He starts wear-
                  ing sweatshirts and sweat pants, a change from
                  the flashy clothes he had worn previously.[78]

Summer 2010   Zahira is born to Karima and Tamerlan.[79]

2010   Tamerlan's wife works up to 80 hours a week to
                  make the $1,200 a month to pay the rent. While
                  she works, Tamerlan looks after their daughter,
                  Zahira. The family's income is supplemented by
                  public assistance and food stamps from Septem-
                  ber 2011 to November 2012.[80]

2010   Tamerlan quits drinking and smoking pot, and
                  starts to pray five times a day, even taking his
                  prayer rug to the boxing gym. At home, he reads
                  Islamic websites, as well as U.S. conspiracy sites,
                  like Alex Jones's InfoWars and Protocols of the
                  Elders of Zion. He says Americans lack values,
                  and stops listening to music out of a belief that it
                  is prohibited by Islam.

January 2011   Pope Benedict condemns violence against
                  Christians in Egypt, calling a car bomb attack
                  "vile and murderous." This, together with previ-
                  ous actions/statements of the pope, leads officials
                  of Cairo's Al-Azhar University, to curtail com-
                  munications with the Vatican.[81]

2011   Tamerlan decides to quit boxing, claiming it
                  was not permitted for a Muslim to hit another
                  man.[82]

2011   In his senior year in high school, Dzhokhar
                  writes a paper on Chechnya.[83]

Early 2011 Russia's Federal Security Service, the FSB, asks the FBI to look into Tamerlan's activities out of concern that he had embraced radical Islam and was going to travel to Russia to join unspecified radical groups. The FBI interviews Tamerlan and his family members and examines his travel and Internet records.[84]

February 2011 Zubeidat becomes more committed to traditional Islam, and soon afterward, she and Anzor split up.

May 2, 2011 Osama bin Laden is killed in a U.S. military operation targeting him in Pakistan.

June 2011 Dzhokhar graduates from Cambridge Rindge and Latin High School. He is awarded a scholarship and also named Most Valuable Player on the wrestling team.[85]

Summer 2011 After interviewing Tamerlan and his family members, the FBI says it "did not find any terrorism activity, domestic or foreign, and those results were provided to the foreign government."[86]

September 2011 Anzor and Zubeidat divorce a few months shy of their 25th wedding anniversary.[87] Their divorce filing cites "an irretrievable breakdown of the marriage." They claim no property, pension, or retirement funds.[88]

2011–13 Tweets from Dzhokhar indicate that he is homesick, has sleep problems including dreams of zombies, and misses his father. During this time, the Tsarnaev sisters have moved away and have gotten married.[89]

September 11, 2011 The 10th anniversary of 9/11 attacks. A friend of Tamerlan and two others are killed in a murder that remains unsolved. Since the bombing, many authorities believe that Tamerlan had something to do with it, though so far there's no hard evidence.[90,91]

September 2011 Anzor leaves for Dagestan, citing ill health and saying that if he is going to die he wants to die there.

September 2011   Dzhokhar enrolls at UMass Dartmouth after
                  receiving a $2,500 scholarship, planning to
                  become a dentist. He then enrolls in engi-
                  neering and switches to biology, saying to
                  some friends that he wants to be a doctor.[92] He
                  smokes a great deal of marijuana, uses other
                  drugs recreationally, plays intramural soccer,
                  and joins the Muslim Student Association on
                  campus.

2011–2013   Dzhokhar sells marijuana, with a successful
                  business. His grades gradually fall from medi-
                  ocre to failing. He spends time with other
                  international students. He is seen as com-
                  passionate and kind to others. He establishes
                  good rapport with the campus police and is
                  warned, but not punished, when found breaking
                  rules.[93]

January 12, 2012 Tamerlan goes back to Dagestan for a six-month
                  visit, leaving from New York. Many Dagestanis
                  have turned toward Salafism, a strict fundamen-
                  talist sect of Islam. Tamerlan's aunt says that in
                  Dagestan he prayed five times a day and went to
                  a Salafist mosque.[94]

Early 2012   Anzor settles in Dagestan and sets up a retail
                  business.[95]

April 15, 2012   Four American Muslim men testify in federal
                  court in Brooklyn. Each had gone to be trained
                  in terror camps by Al Qaeda. Each had been
                  ready to carry out terror attacks in the United
                  States, but had decided not to go ahead with
                  them. They talk about their experiences, and
                  these may shed light on Tamerlan's experience
                  in Dagestan in 2012.[96]

April 16, 2012   Dzhokhar attends Boston marathon as a spec-
                  tator, cheering on the runners.

Spring 2012   Tamerlan, in Dagestan, makes contact with
                  a recruiter named Makhmud Mansur Nidal,
                  through an intermediary named William Plot-
                  nikov. Both these men are killed by authorities
                  while Tamerlan is in Dagestan.[97]

June 13, 2012	Zubeidat is arrested for trying to shoplift up to nine dresses from Lord & Taylor in Natick, Massachusetts.[98] Soon afterward, she leaves for Dagestan.
July 17, 2012	Tamerlan comes back from Dagestan with a full beard.[99] He starts a YouTube channel where he posts recordings with titles like "The End Is Near," "Your Last Day on Earth," and "I Will Dedicate My Life to Jihad."[100] After he returns he loses interest in playing music. He works only sporadically, sometimes delivering pizza, and lives with his wife and child in the Norfolk St. apartment in Cambridge.[101]
Summer 2012	Dzhokhar wants to visit his mother and father, but does not get his U.S. passport in time, so instead he spends the summer lifeguarding at a Harvard pool. He tweets: "Saving lives brings me joy."[102]
August 2012	Dzhokhar, upon learning that $15 billion was spent on the Summer Olympics, tweets: "Imagine if that money was used to feed those in need all over the world," he writes, "The value of human life ain't shit nowadays that's #tragic."
Fall 2012	Dzhokhar returns to college, where he parties in his dorm and lets school work slide.[103] One of his close friends has transferred to another college, another will be leaving soon. Two others have moved off campus. He has difficulties with finances.[104]
September 5, 2012	Tamerlan presents a request for citizenship. The request is deferred, and thus he cannot train for the Olympic boxing team. The application prompted "additional investigation" of him in 2013 by federal law enforcement agencies.[105]
September 11, 2012	Dzhokhar becomes a naturalized citizen of the United States.[106]
2012	Karima and Tamerlan receive welfare payments.[107] Their landlord, Joanna Herlihy, tries to evict them. Zubeidat sends money to Tamerlan

from Russia to help him pay, but in January 2013 they lose their Section 8 rent subsidy.

November 16, 2012   When a preacher at the Islamic Society of Boston mosque says that it is appropriate to celebrate U.S. national holidays such as July 4th and Thanksgiving, Tamerlan stands up and challenges him, arguing that celebrating holidays is "not allowed in the faith." After the sermon, Tamerlan repeatedly argues his viewpoint with the preacher, then leaves.[108]

2012   Reports say that Dzhokhar was desperately trying to grow a beard.[109]

2012   According to a transcript from UMass Dartmouth, reviewed by *The New York Times*, Dzhokhar was failing many of his classes his sophomore year. He was reportedly more than $20,000 in debt to the university.[110]

January 18, 2013   When a preacher at the Islamic Society of Boston mosque says slain civil rights leader Martin Luther King Jr. was a great person, Tamerlan stands up, shouts, and calls him a "nonbeliever." Tamerlan accuses the preacher of "contaminating people's minds" and calls him a hypocrite. People in the congregation shout back at Tamerlan, telling him to "leave now." Leaders of the mosque later tell him he will no longer be welcome if he continues to interrupt sermons. At future prayers, he is quiet.[111]

February 2013   Tamerlan goes to New Hampshire and buys 48 mortars containing approximately 8 pounds of low-explosive powder. Dzhokhar, about this time, downloads a recipe for making a pressure-cooker bomb.[112]

Winter 2013   Dzhokhar downloads onto his laptop some Muslim publications that focus on jihad, including one that has a foreword by Anwar al-Awlaki, an American-born imam who died in a drone attack in 2011. He also downloads a publication called "Make a bomb in the kitchen of your mom."[113]

March 2013	Dzhokhar, home for spring break, hangs out with his usual CRLS friends.[114]
March 18, 2013	Dzhokhar tweets: "People come into your life to help you, hurt you, love you and leave you and that shapes your character and the person you were meant to be."
March 20, 2013	Dzhokhar tweets: "Evil triumphs when good men do nothing."[115] On the same day, Tamerlan and Dzhokhar go to a firing range. They rent two 9mm handguns, buy ammo, and have target practice.[116]
Spring 2013	Dzhokhar drives around with friends who have black BMW with license plate "Terrorista."
April 2013	Two weeks before the bombings, Dzhokhar tells a friend that school is no longer important to him and that the only true things in life are religion and God. He says, "It doesn't matter if you are a doctor or engineer—everybody cheats. . . . With religion and God, you can't cheat."[117]
April 4, 2013	Tamerlan buys electronic components online that could be used to make IEDs.[118]
April 7, 2013	Dzhokhar tweets: "If you have the knowledge and the inspiration all that's left is to take action."[119]
April 11, 2013	Dzhokhar tweets: "Most of you are conditioned by the media."[120]
April 15, 2013	Boston Marathon bombings. Two bombs built out of nails and pressure cookers explode, killing three people and wounding an estimated 264 others.[121] Later in the day, Dzhokhar tweets: "Ain't no love in the heart of the city. Stay safe, people."[122]
April 16, 2013	Sometime after 8 p.m., a friend of Dzhokhar's at the gym notices Dzhokhar sitting on a bench and listening to his iPod. He brings up the bombings. "Tragedies happen," Dzhokhar says. "Tragedies happen like this all the time."[123] In the days after the bombing, reports suggest that Dzhokhar was partying with friends at school.[124]
April 17, 2013	Tamerlan calls his uncle Alvi and says, "I want to have an uncle, and I love you." Tamerlan asks for his uncle Ruslan's number, saying, "I just want to make peace with him." He never calls Ruslan.[125]

April 18, 2013   Police respond to a call on the campus of the Massachusetts Institute of Technology, where university police officer Sean Collier, 26, has been shot. He dies from his injuries. Police later say they believe the bombing suspects were responsible for the shooting.

April 19, 2013   Tamerlan dies after a shootout with police in Watertown, Massachusetts. Dzhokhar is captured later after taking refuge inside a boat in a Watertown yard.

September 18, 2013   Pope Francis reaches out to Grand Imam of Al-Azhar, Ahmed Al Tayeb, of Al Azhar University in Cairo, expressing hope for greater dialogue between Muslims and Christians. This would be a re-establishment of contact that was suspended following some comments made by Pope Benedict in 2006 that were seen as anti-Muslim.[126]

September 21–24, 2013   Attack on Westgate Mall in Nairobi, planned and supported by Al Shabab. Hassan Abdi Dhuhulow is likely one of the attackers. Norwegians worry that their citizens who go to fight in Middle East wars will come home with training and engage in terrorism in Norway.[127]

October 10, 2013   Norwegian PST posts information on its website about its assistance with the investigation into the Westgate Mall attack, for which Al Shabab has taken responsibility.[128]

October 20, 2013   A bus is bombed in a blast in Volgograd, Russia, 400 miles from the planned Sochi Olympics, killing several, including the bomber, a woman who was married to an explosives expert from Dagestan. The blast is thought to have been connected to a threat from a former Chechen rebel to attack the Olympics.[129]

December 15, 2013   *Boston Globe* publishes lengthy article called "The Fall of the House of Tsarnaev," suggesting that the Tsarnaev family's generations of failures, defiance of laws, and psychiatric difficulties were the major factors causing the brothers to engage in terrorism, and that, rather than being influenced by his brother, Dzhokhar played an equal role in the decision and execution of the attacks.[130]

December 29 and December 30, 2013 — Two bomb blasts, one on the 29th and another on the 30th, in Volgograd, kill a total of over 30 civilians. These, like the October 20 blast, are considered likely connected to each other and to an earlier threat to the Sochi Olympics by the Caucasus Emirate, considered to be a terrorist organization. The group also bombed a ski resort in the Caucasus in 2011.[131, 132]

February 2014 — The Winter Olympics begins in Sochi, Russia. Tamerlan had hoped to compete for the U.S. Olympic team there, less than 400 miles from Dagestan, and his father had hoped to attend.

March 28, 2014 — Attorneys for Dzhokhar Tsarnaev assert that the FBI tried to recruit his brother, Tamerlan, to be an informer, reporting on Chechen and Muslim communities.[133]

April 21, 2014 — The 127th Boston Marathon was held in Boston.

2

❖

Nice Young Men and Women Can Create Carnage and Chaos around the World

He was a quiet, polite, good-humored, pleasant and nice kid.[1]

A "charming" person who took an interest in their children.[2]

A charming kid with a bright future.[3]

He was just like other boys. He played football, listened to music, joked with girls.[4]

She was different. She dreamt of becoming a nun.[5]

Five young adults. Each of them seen by others, at least at times, as better than the average young person in human terms. Yet each, evidently willingly, agreed to commit actions designed to cause death, mayhem, and terror among innocent civilians who had personally done nothing to harm them. Their actions were planned and executed on four different continents.[6] We would be wise to learn from their life stories. Why did these good kids not fulfill their childhood dreams? Can we find commonalities among them and others that will help us identify promising youth at risk of becoming terrorists, so we might intervene before it is too late?

If so, what intervention could be effective and accurate, allowing us to prevent good kids from becoming deadly terrorists?

Two of the youth about whom these comments were written, Hassan Abdi Dhuhulow, the "pleasant and nice kid," and Dzhokhar Tsarnaev, the "charming kid with a bright future," have eerily similar childhood stories. Each immigrated to a wealthy Western country from a less-developed one at around age nine. Each came from a country that was racked with violence. Each seemed to assimilate quickly. Each had planned, at one point, to become a physician. Each was successful to a point, and then hit some difficult spots. So far, these stories are not the least bit unusual. Just as Cambridge residents were in shock at the irreversible turns taken in the life of Dzhokhar Tsarnaev, so were Larvik, Norway, residents in shock at the irreversible turn taken in the life of Hassan Abdi Dhuhulow. Gabriel Gatehouse of the BBC called Dhuhulow's home town of Larvik "a sleepy, sleepy place. It's a million miles away . . . in every sense . . . from the ravages of Somalia's 20-year long civil war."[7]

In Tunisia, according to Hayet Saadi, her son, Aymen, was, one year ago, "just like other boys" except that he was an honor student, with excellent grades in his studies of German, English, and History. She speaks out clearly against those who recruited him to a Jihadist cause. "My son was manipulated by criminal bosses, terrorists; he was just an adolescent who talked about jihad."[8]

We could undoubtedly find tens or perhaps hundreds of thousands of young adults whose childhood stories start out this way, but who do not become terrorists. So what happened between the difficult spots and the decision to become terrorists? And are their stories anomalies, or the reflection of a trend?[9]

It seems clear that the "something" that happened to these good kids is that they became radicalized and recruited to sacrifice themselves for a cause. As is the case with the vast majority of youth who become violent, some adult, usually the recruiter, benefits in some way. Those who recruited Dhuhulow and Tsarnaev succeeded insofar as they convinced them to commit to terrorist actions, and Dhuhulow and Tsarnaev carried through with them. But what is the process of recruitment? And if we know about it, how can we effectively intervene? More importantly, how can we see recruitment on the horizon in time to intervene? As will be discussed in Chapter 4, ultimately the goal should be to stop the recruitment process itself—perhaps by making it less desirable to be a recruiter—rather than to inoculate every one of the potential recruits. But that may take some time, and in the meantime inoculating potential recruits may be the best, or only, choice.

WHAT IS KNOWN ABOUT RECRUITMENT?

When we consider recruitment, the similarities between Hassan Abdi Dhuhulow and the older Tsarnaev brother, Tamerlan, share a common process. Like Tamerlan, Dhuhulow was recognized as deviating somewhat from the norm. Like Tamerlan, he was noted to become unusually devout. Like Tamerlan, his level of devoutness and intensity were noticed. Like Tamerlan, Dhuhulow, already somewhat radicalized, made a brief trip back to the country from which he had emigrated. In fact, like Tamerlan, he seems to have returned from that trip even more radicalized. The Norwegian security force was aware of Dhuhulow as being at some risk of recruitment to fighting forces in Somalia, and tried, unsuccessfully, to talk him out of going back to Somalia to join the militia.[10] Similarly, Tamerlan Tsarnaev came to the attention of the Russian, then American security forces. He was questioned by the FBI, but nothing much came of the authorities' efforts, except that they may have led to a delay in Tamerlan's path to U.S. citizenship.[11]

European authorities are becoming concerned about young adults—Westerners from the European Union and the United States, mostly Muslim, although it is possible that the authorities are missing non-Muslims because they are so focused on the Muslim youth—traveling to Syria in particular, but also to other places where there is armed conflict, to fight. It seems that at least 1,000 youth from the EU and North America have already done so, during the two-and-a-half-year war in Syria. It seems very likely that they do so out of a sense of altruism and concern for the victims of the war, as well as for the Syrians who have been living under a regime that the fighters see as repressive. A looming question is whether those who do travel to fight in wars in the Middle East (or elsewhere, such as the Caucasus) are likely to come home and perform terrorist acts in Western countries. Tamerlan Tsarnaev's travel to Dagestan and Hassan Abdi Dhuhulow's to Somalia may be seen in this light, although Tsarnaev returned to perform a terrorist act in the United States, while Dhuhulow evidently participated in a terrorist attack that likely targeted Westerners in Kenya. Perhaps it is not always the choice of the young people who are recruited whether to fight in a foreign place or return home to perform attacks in the Western countries where they live; perhaps their recruiters decide for them.

Surely, in many instances, the person seen by victims as a terrorist is seen by himself or herself as an altruist, acting in support of his or her group, fighting for his or her family, and so on. In other words, the terrorist, in reasoning that is affected by moral disengagement, sees the act as good. The person seen by victims as a terrorist sees himself or herself as a militant or guerrilla or freedom fighter or member of the resistance. It is challenging to grasp that the person who we see as doing a very bad deed may see himself or herself as doing a good deed, albeit that person has to go through some moral disengagement to do so. Perhaps an example that might help Americans is to consider colonists who participated in the American Revolution, whom we see as freedom fighters or guerrillas, but whom the British soldiers might well have seen as terrorists.

When we think of the young men in the Allied Forces during the World War II era, we think of them as heroes and members of the greatest generation. But those heroes killed many innocent civilians and destroyed much of the infrastructure of a country. It is extremely difficult, yet vitally important, if we plan to reduce terrorism by young fighters like Tsarnaev and Dhuhulow, that we understand that they have been led to see their mission as altruistic, heroic, and just as important as we see the mission of our World War II soldiers in relation to saving our own people. While Americans may see these things as being as different as night and day, we ignore the way the young terrorists see them at our great peril.

VARIATIONS ON A THEME

The stories of the other two young adults described in the quotes at the beginning of the chapter vary considerably from those of Dhuhulow, Saadi, and the Tsarnaev brothers. They are not immigrants. Each is living in the country of their birth, while fighting for a cause that was rejected by the official authorities. That is, the violence they volunteered to perpetrate was against the aims of the official governments of their home countries, and for other, nongovernmental groups. Each was part of a group that held not only local but international notoriety as well. The "girl next door" in the second quote is Beate Zschaepe, who is on trial as the last surviving member of a neo-Nazi terror cell accused of murders and bombings designed to scare immigrants into leaving Germany. Now in her 30s, she has been part of a neo-Nazi cell since she was in her teens. The girl who "dreamt of becoming a nun" is a young woman who was a Tamil Tiger, a member in the Liberation Tigers of Tamil Elam (LTTE), in Sri Lanka, a group that is noted for its refinement of the techniques for terrorist acts in which the terrorist dies—so-called suicide bombers. (The LTTE have been responsible for the deaths of some world leaders. For example, the ninth prime minister of the Republic of India, Rajiv Gandhi, was assassinated by LTTE suicide bomber Thenmozhi Rajaratnam on May 21, 1991.) There appear to be fewer commonalities between these two young women than among the three young men. Still, they both were recruited, as adolescents, into lives of violence. And as we examine the lives of these young men and women, we can bet that some adult benefited from their engagement in violent acts. This will be discussed at greater length in Chapter 4.

TSARNAEV AND DHUHULOW: ODD COINCIDENCE OR VANGUARD OF A NEW WAVE OF TERRORISM?

In studying the alleged Boston Marathon bombers and the alleged Westgate attacker, we would be wise to consider that they may represent the vanguard in a wave of violence that their recruiters encourage against Western targets (the Westgate Mall was known as a center that attracted Westerners in Nairobi) by youthful recruits. Activist youth are encouraged to participate within a group or in an entrepreneurial fashion. Based on general patterns of youth and violence, it is safe to assume that the young people who commit these acts are not personally important to their recruiters. The recruiters do not care much about them as people. At best, they are seen as having some sort of connection through a cause. At worst, they are seen as a kind of fodder in the service of a multinational, loosely organized movement in which the recruiters serve as a kind of middle management or human resource department. The recruitment videos that are said to have affected the Tsarnaev brothers were those of a Muslim cleric, Anwar al-Awlaki, formerly an imam in Falls Church, Virginia, who was killed by a U.S. drone in 2011. While one can understand the decision to assassinate this cleric, it is likely that his murder by an American drone gave recruiters a new tool: the videos of an articulate martyr to the cause—one who understood well how to appeal to an American audience.

As Norwegian and other European authorities have said, there is danger that young people who travel to places where they may be trained to fight and kill may then come back home and be a threat to the public. This is similar to a common problem for young former child soldiers in Africa, Asia, and South America, who, once they are released, escape, or are rescued, are often not welcome back in their home villages. While many American parents react with surprise at this, it is important to consider both that the child is now a trained killer, very likely emotionally impaired by the experience, and that the child may also have some enemies, due to the fact that others will identify the child with the militia with which he or she has served. Imagine the families who have little power, who have few resources, and who cannot rely on a functioning legal infrastructure. They are faced with a horrible kind of Sophie's choice—either take back the child who is now a trained soldier, and put the rest of the family at risk, or reject the returning child and protect the rest of the family. The

United Nations and numerous aid organizations are working on protocols for DDR—disarmament, demobilization, and reintegration programs for child soldiers, and many communities have successfully resolved the issue, but the problem is not yet fully solved.

This situation may also resonate with anyone who has known or even read stories about one or more of the 35 or 40 percent of young American soldiers who, after one or more deployments to Iraq or Afghanistan, come home with traumatic stress or traumatic brain injury and have to struggle to resume life outside a war zone. Some of them are, in fact, dangerous to their loved ones, not because they are immoral, but because they have been trained to be killers, and have suffered brain and/or psychological injuries that make it hard to know where they are and who is friend or foe, when they are in the midst of a nightmare or flashback. This is true despite the fact that our Veterans' Administration health care system has the most advanced, effective treatments known for these disorders, and reflects, to some extent, the limits of our knowledge, our treatments, and our technology, as well as the remaining problem of stigma, that makes some of the returning soldiers reluctant to seek mental health care.

At present, we do not have enough information to be sure whether Tamerlan Tsarnaev received specific inspiration, training, or instruction while in Dagestan for six months, and we do not know whether he may even have participated in some violent acts while there. We cannot say for sure that he came back trained to be a killer.[12] We do know that after he returned he was seen as having somewhat extreme religious views, that he openly and publicly criticized other Muslims whose views he thought were not pure enough, and that he listened to online talks by radical clerics. Tamerlan followed the kind of path that the Norwegian authorities worry about, returning from a zone of conflict and posing a threat to security.

The U.S. authorities worry about this too. In April 2012, four young Muslim American men testified in a federal court in Brooklyn regarding the training they received in Al Qaeda terror training camps. They were all told that, with U.S. passports, they were more valuable to the cause because they could commit terrorist acts in the United States, including possibly suicide bombings. They were also told that they could plan a smaller event, and that some plans for larger terrorist attacks fail when smaller ones would succeed. It is likely that Tamerlan received similar instructions, and followed them.[13]

NOT ALL MASS KILLERS ARE TERRORISTS

Why not include Adam Lanza, the 20-year-old who terrorized Sandy Hook Elementary School and killed 26, or Jared Loughner, the 22-year-old who shot Congresswoman Gabby Giffords and killed six in Tucson among the youth who became terrorists? Their actions were not, by definition, terrorism. And that matters, because the analysis of the background and motivations for these actions would likely lead to very different conclusions. For example, police recently released some facts about Adam Lanza, indicating that he was obsessed with school shootings. He did not have, as far as can be told, any political motivation, but rather a troubled mind. Analyzing the factors that go into mass shootings such as that perpetrated by Lanza is a worthwhile endeavor, of course, but it is beyond the scope of this book.

An expert on the study of terrorism, Professor Louise Richardson, of the University of St. Andrews, Scotland, defines terrorism and lists seven criteria for determining whether an act can be called terrorism. For her definition, she says, "Terrorism means deliberately and violently targeting civilians for political purposes."[14] The Westgate attack and the Boston Marathon attack both fit that criterion. Professor Richardson expands on this definition by providing seven criteria. In summary, the act must

1. involve violence or at least the threat of violence,
2. be politically inspired,
3. be an attempt to send a message,
4. have symbolic significance,
5. be the act of substate actors (rather than governments or alliances of governments),
6. use victims as a way of affecting some larger entity, such as an entire country or group, and
7. deliberately target civilians.

While the Boston Marathon bombing and the Westgate Mall attacks fit all these criteria, the actions of Adam Lanza at Sandy Hook Elementary School, and of Jared Loughner, in Tucson, do not. They are not linked to political purposes, or to sending a message, for example.

Based on my own research, I add eighth and ninth criteria. My eighth criterion is that terrorist actors (with very few exceptions) must be sane— even if misguided, seemingly cold-hearted, or vicious. There is virtual consensus among terrorism experts on this point. Successful terrorist actions must be carefully planned and kept secret. Terrorism is not the act of insane, deranged, impulsive, or psychotic thinkers. Most terrorism is performed by groups, albeit sometimes small groups. (As of this writing, there is no publicly available information suggesting that the accused Boston Marathon bombers represented or acted with any larger organization, so their group would be two, although they were inspired by, and may have been supported by, others.) Groups of terrorists would, as experts on the study of terrorism have pointed out,[15] reject or quickly expel members who are psychotic, since they would not be reliable partners; thus, their actions could not be coordinated with others' actions, leading to too much risk of the action failing to be executed as planned. Both Adam Lanza and Jared Loughner, along with various other mass shooters in the course of history, fail to meet the criterion of sanity.[16]

The ninth criterion I add is that terrorist leaders and to a lesser extent their followers must display a specific split in their levels of development in the areas of logistics on the one hand and ideology on the other. The advanced competence and ability to manage complexity in the areas of logistics and organization, as well as executing those plans, allow them to carry out an attack. The immaturity and simple thinking in their ideology allows them to avoid inconvenient ethical dilemmas, such as the dilemma that might arise if they considered the point of view of their victims, or that their actions may radicalize the opposition. My colleague Samuel Sinclair and I have written about this criterion using Al Qaeda leaders as examples.[17] While they were able to plan and carry out the complicated and risky September 11 attacks in the United States, using an international network of semi-autonomous cells, their public pronouncements about good and evil, right and wrong, were concrete and utterly devoid of nuance or complexity.

One could argue that a tenth criterion might be psychopathology, or arrest in the psychological development of the instinct to bond with others, enabling the terrorist to detach from other humans sufficiently to carry out deadly attacks without empathy or guilt. However, it is not necessary to assume psychopathology. In fact, alternative explanations for the ability to kill without guilt are available from social psychology, and are more parsimonious. The best example is the concept of moral disengagement, which is discussed thoroughly in Chapter 3.

CLASSIFYING MODERN JIHADIST TERRORISM

Almost immediately after the Boston Marathon bombing, Charles King wrote that the Boston Marathon bombers were "not your average Chechen Jihadis."[18] In this article, King suggested that the bombings have less to do with the long Chechen struggle for independence, or with Russian attempts to label all Chechens as terrorists. He seems, in the article, to suggest a connection between the Boston Marathon bombings and the war in Syria. That is, he draws the conclusion that many Europeans are concerned that the war in Syria is leading many young people around the world to be, and/or be portrayed as, sympathizers with the

Syrian rebels, and even armed and inspired by those rebels. Like the PST, King seems to be suggesting that Western youth, radicalized by the war in Syria, are likely to pose a threat at home. It seems to me that a few links are missing in that argument.

If we were to compare the Boston Marathon bombing with other recent terrorist actions, it is most like that of the so-called underwear bomber, or that of the so-called shoe bomber, with one important difference: it succeeded. That is, the Boston Marathon bombing was not planned, endorsed, or supported by a large terrorist organization such as Al Qaeda, although Al Qaeda celebrated its success. Indeed, it seems likely that Tamerlan, the older brother, like the so-called shoe bomber, sought to join a larger organization in the Caucuses, but was not welcomed. Such a rejection might well include permission, or even encouragement, to become an entrepreneurial terrorist, in a cruel twist of the anti-nuclear weapon phrase: think globally; act locally.

WHAT ROLE DID IMMIGRATION PLAY IN THE BOSTON MARATHON BOMBINGS?

Immigration may have played a role in two aspects of the Boston Marathon bombings. The role of immigration and the complex psychological challenges it poses are discussed in Chapter 3 in relation to how these may have played a role in the difficult decision making required of Dzhokhar Tsarnaev and Hassan Abdi Dhuhulow when they perceived that their adopted countries were less friendly to Muslims than they might have hoped. In addition, immigration may have played a role in that the American peers of Tsarnaev were evidently naive to the dilemma of identity that immigrant youth face, and seemed to expect Dzhokhar to be fully Americanized. Furthermore, they seemed clueless about the struggles he faced as a member of a family that had suffered due to nothing more than its ethnicity, in the country where he grew up.

Immigration also played a part in terrorism in the United States about 100 years ago, but that was likely because the terrorists had escaped from Europe to the United States. The perpetrators were then called "anarchists" rather than "terrorists."[19] There were multiple events. Notably, on September 16, 1920, "anarchists" bombed the corner of Wall Street and Broad Street in New York City, opposite the headquarters of J. P. Morgan and Company. The description of the aftermath of that lunch-hour bombing, with 38 dead, including four teenage boys, resembles the aftermath of the Boston Marathon bombing. Much later, the bombing was attributed to Italian immigrants. These events fit the criteria for terrorism. They were protests against capitalism, intended by the perpetrators to send a message, and they were perpetrated against innocent civilians.

But one surely does not have to be an immigrant, or be concerned about immigration, to engage in a terrorist action. Indeed, terrorist actions have been perpetrated by non-immigrants in Spain, Sri Lanka, Palestine, Japan, and elsewhere in the 20th and 21st centuries, and these actions do not always have, as their targets, people of an ethnicity, or religion, different from that of the perpetrators. Most terrorist actions are perpetrated by people who believe they have legitimate grievances, and who believe that nonviolent methods of bringing attention to their grievances have not worked and cannot work.

Immigrant status is almost certainly important in the stories of Hassan Abdi Dhuhulow and Dzhokhar Tsarnaev, two young men who immigrated at about the same age, at about the same time period, from war-torn countries to safe and affluent Western ones. Past trauma associated with refugee status may be expressed in unexpected ways, including violence, even generations later; this is discussed at length in Chapter 3.

Chapter 5 discusses ways to reduce or prevent good kids from becoming young terrorists, and addressing the inevitable issues that immigrant youth face is one of the many suggestions. Conversations with a preventive intent would seem to be a necessary start, but it is not clear whether they should be carried out by a national security service, as they were in Norway, or by local authorities. Indeed, it is more likely that friends or family members would be in a better position to change the mind of a young adult trying to find a path toward a meaningful life.

VIOLENCE BACK HOME

While both Dhuhulow and Tsarnaev grew up from about the age of nine in towns that are not characterized by open violence, both had a legacy of violence to contend with. To understand better the atmosphere of violence in Chechnya, I turn to works by Khassan Baiev and Nicholas Daniloff (*Grief of My Heart*)[20] and by Anna Politkovskaya (*A Small Corner of Hell*).[21] Both describe, in excruciating, horrifying detail, the sorts of violence and gruesome scenes that are the legacy of Chechnya's hundreds of years of fighting and resistance to ongoing Russian efforts to annex the state. Politkovskaya was a journalist who traveled through Chechnya, listening to what happened to ordinary citizens during the wars, and reporting it. Her stories were heard in many European cities, where she was invited to speak, but nothing changed. A few years after the publication of the book from which these excerpts are taken, Politkovskaya was killed. Here are a couple of Politkovskaya's descriptions. The first quote describes events in 2002, in the 23rd month of the Second Chechen War, the same year that Dzhokhar and his parents came to the United States from Dagestan.

> And for the hundredth or thousandth cursed time, I hear children in the village streets routinely discussing which fellow villager was found, and in what condition. . . . Today . . . yesterday . . . scalped, with sliced-off ears or chopped-off digits. . . . "So he had no fingers?" one adolescent asks, matter-of-factly. "No, Alaudin had no toes," the other answers apathetically.[22]

In this second section, Politkovskaya is being told by an informant that earlier informants had been killed for talking with her.

> "It's because he told you about the torture. We decided to ask you not to reveal his name anywhere, so his family can survive. And do you remember that black-haired fellow who was sitting in the home-made trestle bed next to the host then? . . . Oh, yes, he kept telling you, 'don't get so upset! We Chechens are tough. I can survive anything.' . . . He's dead too."[23]

Politkovskaya's book, and I suppose her talks, are full of stories of torture and hideous treatment of individuals—children, elders, men, women. These atrocities were being carried out both by militia and by government forces, and the role of government troops was being denied. It is hard to consider.

Baiev's book, by contrast, is not political, but instead portrays the personal journey of a surgeon during the wars. It, too, contains almost unbearable accounts of the pain of civilians in Chechnya during the recent wars. It is also hard to read. As a surgeon, he is called upon to treat victim after victim in an exhausting struggle against death. One cannot come away from Baiev's book without a disturbing awareness of the horrors of war and an appreciation of the incredible luxury of life in a country so far untouched by war within its borders.

During the 1999 war, Baiev was among the few medical personnel working in Chechnya. He writes of one of the most harrowing experiences as a surgeon during this war.

> On the second day, February 1, I operated without a break until about midnight, when I fainted a second time. Again, the nurses rubbed my face with snow, and I went back to work. By the third day, I had performed sixty-seven amputations and seven brain surgeries.[24]

Somalia, like Chechnya, is a country with a history of unrest, chaos, and violence. In November 2013, I put the words "Somalia" and "violence" into a search engine and got 13 million results. A month earlier, Doctors without Borders had announced it would be ceasing to provide services there because armed groups were killing and abducting their workers, and the authorities were either ignoring or supporting this violence.

In areas with high violence and low accountability, everyone is, to a greater or lesser degree, on edge all the time. Even if you feel you are not a likely target, you may have a friend, family member, or colleague who is. And sometimes it doesn't matter because just about anyone could be a target—take the example of Doctors without Borders in Somalia. Common sense would dictate that no one should target them. They are decidedly apolitical, and their mission is to provide health services where no one else is providing them. Yet they felt that, in Somalia, they were being targeted and the governing forces did not help. Perhaps some very hideous and horrifying motivation led one group to hate members of another group so much that they did not want them to get necessary medical care. Hard to believe? Not only does it seem likely this is happening in Somalia, but reading Politkovskaya one cannot escape the conclusion that something hideous and similar was happening in Chechnya during the time she was reporting.

Most youth and adults who emigrate from countries that have a history of violence and unrest do not themselves become violent. And not all violence or terrorism is perpetrated by persons whose heritage is from a violent country. At the same time, countries where there is no effective remedy, and where both the governments and the militia are violent and untrustworthy, and where human rights are violated, create conditions that are more likely to lead to terrorism. Most people growing up in these countries will not condone or join terrorist activities, but if you are seeking the conditions that foster terrorism, look to those factors before things like poverty, unemployment, lack of education, and other common sense explanations.

Sri Lanka during its civil war was an example. Both the Tamil Tiger separatist movement and the government were accused of disappearing, kidnapping, and killing citizens in attempts to gain power and defeat enemies. Ethnic Tamils not only reported unfair conditions where human rights were violated, but they were also able to point to actual laws that favored Sinhalese citizens over Tamils.[25] Asymmetrical warfare followed, with terrorism a tool used by Tamils in an attempt to gain an advantage.

Tamil Tigers launched terrorist attacks on government and civilian installations.

The complex and interacting factors that contribute to the transition from promising young person, from future doctor, nun, or engineer to mass killer are described in detail in Chapter 3, with specific reference to Dzhokhar Tsarnaev. Looking beyond the specific case of the Boston Marathon bombings, and across the continents, it is critical to understand that the countries or political entities most likely to lead to terrorist activity are those in places where human rights are violated, where violence is rampant, and where there is little or no accountability, including no well-functioning legal infrastructure.

These two factors—violations of human rights in the absence of a functional legal infrastructure on the one hand, and public violence on the other—have a common sense connection with the use of terrorist activities to send a message, make a point, or level out an asymmetrical conflict. Terrorism in these contexts can be understood as a somewhat desperate attempt to bring attention to a grievance perceived by the terrorist as legitimate. In countries like Chechnya or Somalia, where the infrastructure has been destroyed by violence, there is no legitimate way to bring attention to grievances or have them addressed. In a country like Sri Lanka, where there is a functional infrastructure, but it functions fairly only for some of the citizens (e.g., the Sinhalese) and does not function fairly for others (the Tamils), Tamils are likely to feel desperate to bring attention to their grievances.

Desperate as they may be, youth in countries like Somalia, Sri Lanka, or Chechnya are not likely to create terrorist activities all on their own. Rather, as will be discussed at greater length in Chapter 4, there is always an adult or group of adults who will benefit from violence who are actively recruiting, kidnapping, threatening, or seducing youth to commit violent actions.

Here we must pause and ask, "Violent in whose eyes?" While we Americans may look to the violence in Chechnya and Somalia with horror, we must also realize that, in some other countries of the world, people view the United States as the most violent of nations, and they have their reasons for doing so, including gun violence and war. This view of the United States is undoubtedly fostered by some who would benefit from being seen as tough and independent of Western influence, such as officials in Afghanistan, Pakistan, and a fair number of countries in the Middle East. In more subtle terms, the United States may be seen by others as exhibiting a kind of violence in its ongoing disproportionate use of the world's resources and its arguably bossy dominance of international relations—which some in the United States think of as American exceptionalism, that is, a special role or responsibility of America to function as the earth's overseer. By still others, within the United States, the country may be seen as exhibiting a kind of violence in its increasing wealth disparities, and diminution of social welfare benefits. Indeed, the Tsarnaev family itself in the last few years experienced a loss of some of the benefits that had enabled them to live as well as they did (see Timeline in Chapter 1). While the United States has a well-functioning legal infrastructure, there is no doubt that it works better for some citizens—namely white, native-born citizens with the means to hire attorneys of their choice—than for others.

So while I will argue that the Tsarnaevs lived in conditions in the United States that were peaceful, in a city that was relatively prosperous, with access to good education and considerable public resources, I will also argue that that is all relative. Compared with the victims of chaos in Chechnya, their life in Cambridge was peaceful, stable, and resource-rich, but compared with that of their Cambridge peers, they might well have been seen as disadvantaged. The living conditions of the Dhuhulow family have not been made public, so I cannot yet say whether they were relatively well-off or poor. Undoubtedly in Norway they had access to some basic social services, such as health services.

VIOLENCE, FEAR, EXCITEMENT, ALTRUISM, AND A MEANINGFUL LIFE

There is one more set of questions to answer about kids who engage in terrorism—what do they like about it? In Sri Lanka, many youth from poor families who could not fully support them, possibly due to having lost the major wage earner in war, found, in the Tamil Tigers, a kind of family and home that had better resources than their own family did. Supported from within Sri Lanka and from expatriates who had done well, the Tamil Tigers were able to provide necessities to their recruits. Perhaps equally importantly, and clearly true for militia that recruit volunteers around the world, the Tamil Tigers helped provide a life that was, in a misguided way, meaningful to the youth engaged in it. Beyond a meaningful life, it promised them fame, recognition, and appreciation forever. That is, those who died for the cause of a separate and independent land for Tamils within the island of Sri Lanka were promised that they would be recognized and celebrated every year, in perpetuity. Comparing that with the odds of getting an education or a decent job, some youth decided that death for a cause was a better choice. They also believed, again in a misguided way, that by dying they were providing a chance at freedom and a better life for their families.

We do not, in the United States, have military missions where soldiers agree in advance and plan to die in order to succeed at causing harm to the enemy's forces, and/or reducing the likelihood that the enemy will harm Americans. If we did, I can imagine that there would be young men and women who would, after weighing the odds, volunteer for such missions. What would differentiate them from those who would not do so? Once we fully understand that, we will have taken another step toward reducing terrorism. A commonsense hunch would be that they would be men and women who had no children, but who might have sisters, brothers, nieces, nephews. They might not have a romantic partner, or the relationship might not have promise. They might have recently lost loved ones, and feel that they could be reunited with them in an afterlife. Those are common sense ideas, but I predict that the answers will defy common sense. Many terrorists believe that they would be gaining entry into heaven for their altruism. I can imagine a young recruit thinking, "Greater love hath no man than this, that he lay down his life for his friends."[26] Still others might be willing to die in a mission if they felt that it was necessary in order to avenge the death of a loved one. Both loyalty and revenge are powerful motives.

But most youth engaged in violence around the world have been kidnapped, forced, recruited, or seduced into fighting someone else's war, and are deceived into thinking they are fighting of their own free will, or that there is pride and reward for fighting bravely, or that it makes their lives more meaningful. Some would probably imagine a special place in hell for terrorists. I would reserve a special place in the hell of my imagination for those who recruit youth to immersion in violence.

As I completed this book, the world grieved Nelson Mandela, who died on December 5, 2013, at the age of 95. Mandela, recognized as special beginning in his childhood, is now recognized as an extraordinarily moral and admirable person, responsible, with a handful of others, for the end of apartheid and for radical changes in South Africa that are universally recognized as progress. But he was once considered to be a terrorist, and that should give us all pause. What does it mean that a person who, as a child was seen as destined for great things, then joined an organization that much of the world saw as terrorists? Indeed what shall we make of the fact that he was on the U.S. terrorist list until removed in 2008, long after the world recognized him as a great peaceful leader? What shall we make of the fact that, offered release from prison in exchange for renouncing violence as a tool, he declined? After 27 years in prison, he became, in his later years, a leader, president, a force for peace, a winner of the Nobel Peace Prize, and more importantly a man who symbolized, in his own life, willingness to suffer and sacrifice not only for justice, but for inclusiveness. Yes, he was special. As President Obama said, "We will not likely see the likes of Nelson Mandela again."[27] But many did not see him as special, at least not in a good sense, during his terrorist years. Is it possible that some day we will see some of the grievances of today's young terrorists as justified? And that some day we will see some of those young terrorists become leaders in the worldwide struggle for peace and justice?

3

Many Factors Contribute to the Decision to Resort to Violence

"The U.S. Government is killing our innocent civilians"; "I can't stand to see such evil go unpunished"; "We Muslims are one body, you hurt one you hurt us all"; "Now I don't like killing innocent people it is forbidden in Islam but due to said [unintelligible] it is allowed"; and "Stop killing our innocent people and we will stop."[1]

Marathon victims like collateral damage in wars in Afghanistan and Iraq . . .[2]

I do not mourn my brother's death because now Tamerlan is a martyr in paradise and I expect to join him in paradise.[3]

Fuck America.[4]

People who kill in spite of the inhibitions and penalties that confront them are people moved by strong passions.[5]

By now everyone who has been following the story of the Boston Marathon bombings has read the first four quotes above, text written by Dzhokhar inside a boat in a resident's driveway in Watertown, Massachusetts, on April 19, 2013, where he was hiding following events of the evening of the 18th and morning of the 19th of April 2013, when the two Tsarnaev brothers allegedly killed an MIT police officer, hijacked a car and held the driver hostage, and had a shootout with numerous police officers, in which they attempted to use bombs similar to those used in the Marathon bombing against the police. They were evidently on their way to New York City, carrying more pressure-cooker bombs, hoping to explode them at Times Square, but that plan was foiled by police. Tamerlan was killed in the fight, and Dzhokhar, injured, fled, and hid in a boat. The entire town of Watertown, as well as surrounding towns, was on lockdown that day. Travel in the surrounding towns was discouraged. The Boston subway and bus system was shut down. Businesses and schools were closed. Meetings were cancelled. All this was done in an attempt to keep civilians safe and give police the ability to quickly apprehend Dzhokhar, whose whereabouts were in question, but who was eventually found hiding in a boat in a resident's back yard in Watertown.

These musings of a young man who evidently anticipated death, though he must have understood that he might be discovered alive, give us a window into the motivation for the bombings. Experts had already been asserting that Islam, rather than Chechnyan independence issues, was likely the motivation.[6] In some respects, Dzhokhar's case is like that of a growing list of young Muslim Americans, told by recruiters that attacks on Americans are the most effective means to express their loyalty to Islam and to others of their faith, and their disapproval of their adopted Christian country's seemingly endless alliance with Israel and seemingly endless wars and attacks on Muslim countries such as Iraq, Afghanistan, and Pakistan. Some of those young men tried and failed to launch an attack, such as the shoe bomber, or the underwear bomber, or the Times Square bomber, none of whom caused the deaths or havoc intended. Others have simply changed their minds, like the men who testified in 2012 in a Brooklyn court.[7]

In Chapter 4, we will examine this pattern of adults who try to recruit younger men and women to perform violent actions that put the younger men or women, but not the adults, at risk. In fact all too often the older adults stand to gain money, power, or fame as a result of their actions. This pattern is not limited to Muslims, and not even to terrorist attacks. Numerous commentators and scholars have pointed out that the way to stop such violence is to focus on the people who benefit, rather than on the people who perform the violent actions.

At the same time, people in and around Cambridge want to know more specifically about Dzhokhar. Sure there are adults trying to recruit young Muslims to engage in violence, but why did this particular young man whom the people of Cambridge knew and loved, who had so much promise, and who could have done great things, fall prey to the influence of recruiters? Even if his brother played a role, it is almost unfathomable to most of those who knew Dzhokhar that he would actually kill, maim, and harm people knowingly. This chapter focuses on how Dzhokhar likely became vulnerable to recruitment. Perhaps what we learn from this will help us intervene in the lives of some other young men and women who may be vulnerable to recruitment. Maybe we can find a way to inoculate them—warn them in advance—that some day they may be tempted. Much as African American families warn their children about the likelihood of being detained, stopped and frisked, questioned, treated unfairly, accused, and viewed with suspicion, and train them about the best way to act and react, perhaps methods can be developed to train young men and women to resist the temptation to be recruited to perform religiously based violence.

This is a familiar task. Much like we want to teach young people to resist situations that are risky in terms of sex or drugs, perhaps we have to add to that list the necessity of training them to resist recruitment. Perhaps talking them out of it near the point of departure, as the Norwegian PST has attempted, is too little, too late.

WHAT DOES PSYCHOLOGY HAVE TO DO WITH A YOUNG MAN'S DECISION TO KILL, MAIM, AND DESTROY THE LIVES OF INNOCENT PEOPLE WHO HAD DONE NOTHING TO HIM PERSONALLY?

Psychologists have been idealized, scorned, and contradicted when trying to analyze behavior. Sadly, we often radically disagree among ourselves, especially when we try to understand behavior from a strictly clinical point of view, seeing psychopathology alone as determining behavior. Psychopathology does not determine behavior, and clinical psychologists like me have no special window into that reality. In fact psychopathology is a fairly weak element in a large picture of what determines behavior. Another fairly weak window is personality. Neither of these alone determines behavior, although they both contribute. The two areas of psychology that best explain behavior are social psychology, which calls on the power of the situation to affect behavior, and developmental psychology, which calls on the level of development, or capacity to analyze complex problems, to explain a person's behavior. The following psychological principles have been drawn from those two psychological frameworks. Political psychology and behavioral economics are also factors to contend with. People often act out of economic and political (popularly termed enlightened) self-interest. While we cannot yet draw out a full analysis of Dzhokhar from these frameworks alone, we can use them to make educated guesses about what did, and did not, happen that contributed to the fateful decision he is accused of making, to explode pressure-cooker bombs in the midst of innocent noncombatants and, in doing so, create a chapter in a story that seemed, to him at least, to be about the West's tendency in recent years to have wars with Muslim countries. The same story seemed to most Bostonians, and most Americans, to be about the tendency of young foreigners to be untrustworthy. Unfortunately, that version of the story is apt to cause more harm to young, foreign-born Americans than the Boston Marathon bombs did to innocent bystanders. Because of the prejudice and hatred generated by this version of events, some immigrants, including young professionals, have already been targeted, bullied, threatened, and harmed. Many more will likely be traumatized by threats and attacks by impaired individuals who think that all immigrants are suspect.

The goal of this book is to reduce terrorism, and reduce prejudice against foreign-born, young Americans, simultaneously. Contemporary world events are challenging enough, without allowing recruiters to gain wealth, fame, and power by encouraging young men and women to kill and maim innocent civilians. Can psychology do that? Yes, it can, if we can avoid the tendency to accept simple explanations, whether psychological or not, and can be patient enough to explore multiple factors contributing to the psychology of a good kid's decision to become a deadly terrorist.

The following sections describe psychological principles that help us understand Dzhokhar and others like him. No single one of these principles alone accounts for his actions, but each of them plays a role, and taken together they go a long way toward explaining how Dzhokhar—a good kid, a popular graduate of an American high school, beloved by teachers, coaches, and peers—ended up writing "Fuck America" inside a boat while awaiting death or arrest.

PARENTAL INATTENTION OR NEGLECT

Psychologist Laurence Steinberg has studied at-risk adolescents for decades, and his exhaustive review of studies, as well as his own research, points to a variety of commonalities. While it is not true of every adolescent who gets into trouble, the difficulty found more commonly than others by researchers in the United States is lack of parental engagement, spanning from parents who are too busy or unable to pay enough attention to their adolescent children to parents who are downright neglectful.[8] Various reports of the Tsarnaev family, most notably a December 2013 article in *The Boston Globe*, suggest that Dzhokhar's parents, Zubeidat and Anzor, were preoccupied with many concerns, not the least of them providing for their family, to be consistently available to their children as the children got older. Perhaps more dramatic, and more puzzling, the parents appear to have been strongly engaged with and ambitious for the older of the brothers, Tamerlan, at the cost of the other children. Reports from Dzhokhar's wrestling coach, in particular, indicate that no one from the Tsarnaev family ever attended matches or accompanied him when he won the Most Valuable Player award. Of course, very few kids whose parents are unavailable to support them go on to become terrorists. This lack of attention is not the cause of Dzhokhar's actions. But it is likely a factor, as it may be a factor with other kids who get recruited to terrorism.

MORAL DISENGAGEMENT

This principle, well supported by research, explains how a person can "turn off" the internal moral compass that would generally tell the right way to act in a certain situation. There are several mechanisms that a person can use that will enable him or her to act in a way that violates his or her own usual values. For example, a soldier who, in everyday life, would never dream of killing anyone can override that value in wartime by telling himself or herself that in this situation, the person or persons being killed are a threat to the soldier's family or a threat to society or really less than human.[9] Other ways a person may become morally disengaged include by seeing himself or herself as obeying orders, by a kind of assumption that everyone in the reference group is killing or justifying killing, or by not thinking about the consequences of his or her actions. When the Tamil soldier in Chapter 2, when interviewed in the film,[10] says that her leader would not "choose anything that causes devastation to civilians," she is using two methods of disengagement: turning responsibility over to her leader and misrepresenting civilian victims to herself. Note here that others may have deliberately planned their activities and words to convince or encourage the Tamil soldier to morally disengage, but the actual disengagement is an internal act. However, she may have been more vulnerable to being convinced because of her youth, and because of cultural norms dictating that youth defer to elders, leading to greater amenability to influence by an older, charismatic leader.

In explaining the process by which people move from dissatisfaction with the status quo to terrorism, Fathali Moghaddam provides an excellent illustration of how moral disengagement works at several levels in the transition.[11] The steps Moghaddam outlines include, in order, (1) being aware of grievances and systematic unfairness, (2) blaming a powerful, external entity, (3) believing that the only potentially successful way to address the grievances is through violence, and thus justifying violence as a means to a desired end, (4) developing an in-group identity that defines the other as the enemy, and (5) believing that by a personally self-sacrificing, heroic act, one will be doing good for the world.[12, 13]

THIRD CULTURE KIDS

Third culture kids (TCKs) are an ever-increasing group of youth who are growing up in a culture that is not the culture of their parents. Many TCKs feel as if they have two cultures and no culture. They wonder where they belong or lament that there is nowhere they belong. Pollock and Van Reken describe them in the following way:

> TCKs are raised in a neither/nor world. It is neither fully the world of their parents' culture (or cultures) nor fully the world of the other culture (or cultures) in which they were raised. Contrary to popular misconceptions, however, this neither/nor world is not merely a personal amalgamation of the various cultures they have known. . . . [I]n the process of living first in one dominant culture and then moving to another one (and maybe even two or three more and often back and forth between them all), TCKs develop their own life patterns different from those who are basically born and bred in one place. Most TCKs learn to live comfortably in this world, whether they stop to define it or not.[14]

The word "most" here is key, for it is clear from the tweets and messages of Dzhokhar Tsarnaev that he did not live comfortably in his world. It seems that partying and smoking a great deal of marijuana may have helped him enough during high school, while community, school, and parental support were available to him, but as these fell away, the fault lines of his tenuous internal ability to "live comfortably" in this world became increasingly evident. Historical, political, and cultural considerations were also in play for a young man whose religion was subject to misunderstanding, stereotyping, and hatred by many in his adopted country. In addition, his own ethnic identity as Chechen was too often linked with terrorism or suicide bombers. Note that difficulties of this nature are not unique to Dzhokhar, and are not uncommon among TCKs.

> Although their expanded worldview is a great benefit, it can also leave TCKs with a sense of confusion about such complex things as politics, patriotism, and values. Should they support the policies of

their home country when those policies are detrimental to their host country? Or should they support the host country even if it means opposing policies of their own government?[15]

These questions are ever more complex in a world where alliances between and within countries are ever-changing, and where in many instances of conflict, nonstate actors such as Al Qaeda, Shining Path, Fuerzas Armadas Revolucionarias de Colombia, ETA, Hamas, and the Irish Republican Army have launched offensives against one another or against state actors. Examples inside Chechnya seem to illustrate this phenomenon:

Over the past decade, the more moderate, secular figures in the original Chechen resistance were purposefully ignored by Moscow and pushed aside by more extremist fighters. Today's conflict is a grinding civil war fuelled in equal parts by the more violent strains of Salafi Islam and a toxic cycle of never-ending revenge killing. Across the whole of the North Caucasus, the police battle militants that are organised into jamaats, local cells that range in size and sophistication from a few teenagers watching jihadi videos at home to organised and hierarchical militias.[16]

Another example is Palestine, where several rival factions that are not simply political parties have coexisted, sometimes fighting one another, and, it seems, independently had better or worse relationships with neighboring states.[17]

In contemporary times, one can be identified not only with multiple states, but also with multiple nonstate organizations, some of which are essentially at war with states and with other nonstate organizations. In this context, one's allegiance to one state, one religion, or one organization is not necessarily static. According to multiple developmental psychology theories and studies, late adolescence is a time when youth in the United States are likely to be very actively considering who they are and what they might be committed to. More advanced studies reflect that each of us has multiple identities—gender, race, ethnicity, religion, family, culture, career, avocational interest, and so on. In any given setting, one or more of these might be more salient than the others. For example, one might be a Red Sox fan on a Wednesday evening, and a professor on Thursday morning. But for TCKs, when culture, ethnicity, home country, and even religion are salient, it can be an unsettling experience. Which culture, which *side in this conflict* do I identify with? If my home country is attacking the country my parents chose to immigrate to, where is my allegiance?

It would be hard to overestimate the challenges associated with this dilemma, and the need for young adults to have a chance to explore and hold these multiple identities simultaneously while formulating answers to such vexing questions.

Indeed, successful, well-educated Canadian rapper Shad, born in Kenya of Rwandan parents, who immigrated with his family to Canada, says in notes accompanying the release of his recent album, *Flying Colours*:

> The innumerable stories that comprise our treasured multiculturalism here in Canada can also hold a lot [of] pain, as well as some complicated questions around what it means to succeed, and what it means to belong.[18]

Shad also addresses these issues in one of the songs on the album, "Fam Jam." The lyrics include the following:

> Now when you're Third World born, but First World formed
> Sometimes you feel pride, sometimes you feel torn.[19]

Both of these would seem to apply to Dzhokhar, as well as to Hassan Abdi Dhuhulow, the Norwegian mentioned in Chapter 2, who had immigrated from Somalia, and who was one of two men named as West Gate mall attackers in a January 2014 trial of four men accused in connection with the attack. The trial took place in Nairobi.[20]

MULTIPLE IDENTITIES AND CODE SWITCHING

Most mainstream adults in the United States can identify with the adolescent feeling of not knowing quite who they are, how they are seen, or what they want to be. Child or adult? Funny or serious? Attractive or not? Sexy or intellectual? Jock or nerd? Still, it is harder for most mainstream Americans to understand the intense and sometimes overwhelming feelings of kids for whom some of the multiple identities or aspects of themselves represent—and are parts of—groups that hate one another. On an individual level, you might think of a child whose parents perhaps divorced and whose parents' families, hate one another and are in constant conflict. On a larger scale, think of a bi-racial child who experiences two families on different sides of the great American racial divide. And many kids live different lives with their American peers, and are fully accepted by those peers with the pretense that they are no different. At home they speak a language, eat foods, and live by rules that are all different from those of their American peers. And what if the language, culture, religion, food, and lifestyle patterns of their family are denounced, looked down upon, mocked by their American peers? What if their ethnicity, or race, is considered to be dirty, lazy, stupid, or violent?

Kids who live these multiple lives learn to switch, in a manner of speaking, to leave one of their language, racial, ethnic, and religious, selves at the door when they enter the space occupied by the other. This is known as code switching. But that only goes so far. For some kids, in each space they hear their loved ones from the other space denigrated, or idealized, but never understood.

For some kids, there are several identities: the identity they take on, and display, with their mainstream peers; the identity they take on, and display, with their non-mainstream family; the identity when in public, where they are mistrusted, misperceived, or devalued. For some kids, every step into the public domain is risky. They may be stopped by a police officer and frisked or detained. If they are Muslim, the Federal Bureau Investigation (FBI) may invite them in for a "voluntary" interview. Even if they are young, hopeful, and full of energy, these things can take a toll, wear them down, remind them that they have a burden that others may not have.

Perhaps they are TCK who have experienced war and are refugees, along with their family. In their parents' country, they saw and heard some grisly things and understood a level of hatred and unfairness that would be unbelievable to their American peers. How do they deal with it? Many such kids simply bury their memories—assuming their American peers, sheltered and privileged, could never begin to fathom what they have seen and perhaps also appreciating an opportunity to avoid thinking about the past.

So for TCKs from war-torn countries, the split in their identities is likely to be more prominent, more complete, and more damaging, because one of the clearest findings about trauma and posttrauma stress is that talking about the trauma and integrating it as part of our history and biography is an important part of healing.

SINGLE IDENTITY

While holding onto multiple identities may be challenging, it seems that no matter how many identities we juggle and try to integrate, others may see us as having only one identity. For example, when African Americans in the United States interact with another person—especially if that person is white—the one identity that will stand out is their race. The other person may fail to see them in all their complexity, and instead stereotype them based on their expectations—right or wrong—and their perceptions—right or wrong—of the inherent qualities of people of their race. Perhaps they will assume African Americans are lazy, not bright, and likely to rob them. Asian Americans, people assume, are good at science and math, and are precise, patient, and poised. Jewish are assumed to be rich, look out only for their own, and might, at worst, try to cheat others for money. People see Muslims, no matter what else they are—say, a soccer player, or a physician, or a banker, or an artist, a mother, daughter, son, father, uncle, or grandparent—as a Muslim first and fore-most. And, in the United States, people may fear them and assume they are violent terrorists.

To be clear, every person has multiple different identities. Most of the time, those identities exist simultaneously, and do not come into conflict. Different identities are salient in different contexts. For example, a fic-tional character we can call "Cassandra" may be a cyclist, tennis player, author, teacher, coach, member of a book group, sister, daughter, mother, alumna of a specific high school and college, donor, volunteer, and condo owner. And she may also be a Muslim. At different moments, one or another of those identities is salient. But they are all part of her at any given time. Suppose Cassandra, at one of her condo meetings, is confronted by a neighbor who is really upset at having learned that Cassandra has been having friends over for religious discussions. The neighbor is worried that Cassandra's friends are plotting against the condo association, or planning a violent attack. Having known Cassandra for years, the neighbor knows that Cassandra is a mother, daughter, teacher, and responsible community member. But once she hears that Cassandra is meeting with other mem-bers of her faith, the neighbor can only focus on that one single identity.

This dangerous reality of being seen as having a single identity is matched by the danger of a single story.

SINGLE STORY

The concept of a single story is the group equivalent of a single iden-tity. And, just as the attribution of a single identity has problems for the individual, the attribution of a single story has consequences for a group. After September 11, 2001, attacks, not only all Muslims, but also a lot of people who simply had brown skin, or spoke with slight accents, were seen as potentially dangerous. They were shunned by neighbors. Their children were bullied. They had a harder time getting jobs. And they were endlessly stopped and detained at airports and at the border. Reporter Sarah Abdurrahman reported on how she, her husband, and many of their friends, American citizens, were stopped and detained while traveling home from a wedding in Canada. ACLU attorneys verified, in this piece, that American citizens are frequently stopped, not given any reason for being stopped, and detained for long periods of time. Repeated efforts to investigate the rights of citizens and the procedures from the Customs and Border Patrol agency were unsuccessful.[21]

Another good example of the dangers of a single story is the treatment of LGBT (lesbian, gay, bisexual, and transgender) groups in the United States, because we can actually see changes reflecting the shifting from a single rigid story to a set of flexible and much more interesting stories. This change is perhaps best reflected in the fact that many states have begun to recognize same-sex marriages, all within the last 10 or so years. Prior to that, gay and lesbian couples were not seen as stable, committed, monogamous couples. Many imagined that children raised by such couples would be disadvantaged, when compared to those raised by heterosexual couples, despite a great deal of high-quality social science research indicating that children raised in gay and lesbian households did just as well as those raised in heterosexual households. Somehow the single story had blocked many mainstream adults, including those with the power to make decisions about custody and about adoption, from hearing the results of that research. In Chapter 5, we address in more detail how the problem of a single story can be successfully addressed, using this as an example. Once freed from the single story attributed to them, those who were the objects of the single story can make a wider range of choices, and can be seen in their complexity.

Single stories can be rather insidious, as noted in the TED talk by Chimamanda Ngozi Adichie.[22] She provides multiple examples of how she and others made assumptions based on the single stories they had been told and had never questioned. These single stories created one-dimensional images of others who were, of course, more complex. They also omitted some real people from some real situations where, it seemed from the single story, they could not belong. For example, Adichie wrote a novel whose characters were drawn from her experience in a middle-class Nigerian family. She was then told by her professor that the characters were not "authentically African" because they did not fit the professor's stereotyped perception of Africans who were starving and would not be driving cars. Not only were her characters seen as inauthentic, but real African people like herself—people whom she knew and loved—were, she learned, confusing to Americans.

As we will see, Dzhokhar's Cambridge friends had a single story about him. That he was chill, very smart, and just like them, a real Cambridge kid, fully assimilated, and with a past in a faraway country—a past that was irrelevant to his current life. Some of them also likely had a single story about immigrants as foreigners—different—that Dzhokhar did not fit. Overall, then, they ended up not seeing much of who he was. As Janet Reitman's article indicated, they did not see his pain. They did not see his past, or, evidently inquire about it. They did not inquire about the languages he spoke, or the cultures he knew. They seemed to know nothing about his past in Kyrgyzstan or his past in Dagestan, or his family's past in Chechnya. They did not seem to see him in his complexity. In that blindness, they unintentionally failed Dzhokhar, leaving him to struggle alone to integrate his multiple identities.

At the same time, members of his family had a different story—one that hardly overlapped, it seems, with the single story that his friends held. It appears, from interviews with friends and family members, that his parents, Anzor and Zubeidat, were quite involved with Dzhokhar's older brother Tamerlan, and that they may even have idealized him.

> My Tamerlan was a really, really beautiful boy. Handsome like Hercules. Tall and beautiful. His body was like "oh my God," like, written. You know, shedevr [masterpiece]. So it is not possible not to know the body of my child.[23]

Dzhokhar, it seems, was seen as the young and somewhat innocent brother, loved by his older brother. Both Dzhokhar's mother and his brother seem, in recent years, to have believed that Dzhokhar was in need of discipline and information that would cause him to become more devout and far more familiar and more highly identified with his Muslim heritage. His mother tried to encourage him to stop smoking marijuana, apparently, as he notes in one of his tweets that she smelled his hair when he came in. She even tried, according to one of his tweets, to arrange a marriage for him, but he declined.

What his friends and family appear to have in common in their view of Dzhokhar is that he was easygoing. From our current perspective we might see this as a kind of external chameleon style. It helped him to fit into a variety of contexts, but it also hurt him, in that it seems no one really knew him in his complexity; rather, each person saw the facet of him that filled his or her needs. The friends and teachers and coaches did not draw him out. Perhaps that would be a lot to expect of his friends. But it is not so clear whether the teachers or coaches should have tried harder to get

Dzhokhar to talk about who he was in all his complexity. It seems likely that teachers, coaches, and students felt it was important to respect his privacy. But privacy does not always reflect strength. Perhaps the teachers took his privacy too seriously.

Dzhokhar's initial reaction to Tamerlan seems to have been to outwardly comply with expectations, while inwardly resisting his efforts. Gradually, however, Dzhokhar began to see things as his brother desired. Outward compliance seems to have been Dzhokhar's style. He outwardly complied with friends, with teachers' expectations, with his brother's wishes.

It was likely easier for Dzhokhar to resist his mother's and brother's efforts to get him to be more closely identified with Islam while his father was living in the household, because his father was also a believer in a more relaxed form of Islam, as had been practiced in Chechnya for generations. In this respect, the Tsarnaev household paralleled the situation in the Caucasus, where there was, and is, an ongoing struggle between two forces: one encouraging a devout, perhaps fundamentalist, form of Islam (mostly inspired by youthful travelers from the Middle East, who have been exposed to a kind of jihadi perspective), and one favoring a more moderate and relaxed form of Islam—one that defines values and roles, but does not look to violent tactics. Indeed this struggle is now a rather violent one. It seems that those who favor the more extreme, Salafist Islam have, as a goal, the establishment of a religious state that would combine Dagestan and Chechnya into one entity.

So Dzhokhar was likely seen by his family as an innocent young man who was less devout than his brother and mother were, and who was becoming somewhat—perhaps overly—assimilated. His friends and teachers, it seems, just saw him as a typical American peer, a friend, easygoing, carefree, chill.

While teachers may have been Dzhokhar's right to privacy too seriously, it seems even more likely that his friends, teachers, and coaches failed to take his habit of smoking a lot of marijuana seriously enough.

MARIJUANA, COGNITIVE FUNCTIONING, DECISION MAKING, AND DEPRESSION

Looking back at Dzhokhar's tweets, and considering the year or so before the marathon bombing, it is easy to recognize how helpful it would have been for him to be clear-thinking, to have optimal decision-making abilities, to have a well-developed ability to self-reflect, and to have the benefit of talking to multiple peers and mentors as he considered the typical tasks of emerging adulthood in the United States—specifically, going from understanding the world in black-and-white terms to understanding it in terms of multiple realities, and making a commitment to a set of beliefs and a path in life. In his case, this might have meant initially trying to understand which of the religious approaches—his brother's or father's—was right. And it might also have applied to whether the American government's approach toward Middle Eastern countries was good or bad. Perhaps, with multiple opportunities to talk with trusted others, he might have moved toward seeing that the world was not—despite the words of pundits, politicians, or religious zealots—so easy to divide into right or wrong, and that there was not a fundamental inconsistency among the Abrahamic religions. Perhaps, one might hope, he could have seen that he was free to make a commitment of his own, and that that commitment need not be to a black-and-white reality. He might not have needed to see Cambridge people as "fake as fuck" or to see 9/11 as having been an inside job. He might have held these possibilities for a while, giving himself time to decide what he, Dzhokhar, would stand for. Instead it seems that these tasks were rushed, perhaps by the urgency of Tamerlan's deteriorating financial state, and there was no one who knew Dzhokhar's dilemmas well enough that he could confide in, to get support while he delayed choosing sides, knowing that neither side had the one and only truth. Similar tasks were articulated by Dr. William Perry, in his studies of Harvard students in the mid-20th century, and Perry's theory seem to have stood the test of time.

Multiple accounts of Dzhokhar's adolescence in Cambridge, as well as the years in college, indicate that he was a heavy smoker of marijuana, heavier than his Cambridge peers, among whom smoking marijuana is a common activity. I do not argue here that marijuana should be more heavily regulated than it is now. Similar, perhaps, to alcohol, recreational and modest use causes no harm to most people, but heavy use carries risks. All indications that I could find suggest that Dzhokhar was not a recreational user, but rather that his use of marijuana was problematic.

While marijuana may serve many useful purposes, especially in helping patients with cancer who need to cope with the side effects of chemotherapy, heavy use does not enhance clear or focused thinking, and it does not help with decision making. Indeed, it impairs both of those.

The impact of heavy marijuana use during adolescence is still being explored, but the overall results point to association with some aspects of impulsive behavior, including poorer decision making, though it is not clear whether the poorer decision making is a result of the marijuana use, or of other problems that may lead to both marijuana use and poorer decision making.[24]

The possible impact of impaired decision making would not seem likely to be applicable to a major decision, evidently made over several months, such as whether to bomb the Boston marathon. However, according to Moghaddam and many other experts on the study of terrorism, neither the decision to engage in a terrorist action nor the decision to join an organization that engages in terrorism is made in one step.[25] Rather, the decision is actually made of many smaller decisions, each making the next decision easier. Such small steps might well require the clearest thinking possible.

REFUGEE STATUS

Recent literature and documentary videos have painstakingly recorded and reflected the anguish of refugees in the United States and around the world. Refuge is a very positive word, suggesting peace, safety, and protection. But refugees in the United States typically experience none of these. Although they may be safer here than in their home countries, initial financial challenges offer limited housing choices, and they often end up having to live in neighborhoods where frequent violence is a constant reminder of the lack of peace and the dangers they were trying to escape from in their home countries. Most refugees in the United States feel very little protection, except if they are fortunate enough to receive help from kind strangers, such as religious and civil resettlement programs. Resettlement case managers are constantly stressed by their desire to accomplish the herculean task of actually guiding refugees toward the resources they need to fulfill the promise of a better future for their children.

Just to clarify, refugees and asylees are both immigrants who have experienced danger in their home countries and sought safety in a different country. Refugees apply to the United Nations for status and an opportunity to immigrate to a safe country that is willing to accept them. Asylees apply to a specific country, from inside that country, after somehow having gotten to the country, perhaps entering as tourists. The Tsarnaevs came to the United States and sought asylum here based on their experience of persecution as Chechens in Kyrgyzstan, during the second of the recent Chechen wars. Easy as this sounds—and for some high-profile people it may be fairly easy—for most people, the journey from danger to safety is long, arduous, and ultimately disappointing. Many European countries and the United States are engaged in internal conversations and conflict about whether to accept refugees and how many to accept. Displaced persons (people who have fled war, but who have not yet achieved refugee status) from the current Syrian war are having a particularly hard time with attempts to settle in Lebanon, Bulgaria, and other countries that might be safer than Syria.

The average length of time it takes from when an individual receives status as a refugee from the UN to the time he or she arrives in the new host country is a stunning 17 years. Many who have refugee status live in refugee camps for that long. Seeking asylum, a more risky approach, can still take several years, with less likelihood of success in being allowed a path to citizenship in the new country. The transition is not easy, and making one's way in a new host country poses difficulties that are, for some, insurmountable. Many people who are professionals in their home country come to the United States and are unable to practice because they are unable to become fluent enough in English and/or to repeat their education and training here, at their own expense—which is usually prohibitive. They are not alone in being disappointed in their inability to support themselves, or in the biases against them—based on language, religion, ethnicity, poverty, immigrant status, or any one of many such factors.

Disappointment and grievances—justified or not—loomed large for the Tsarnaev family, who, it seems, came to the United States to escape persecution and also with hopes—for a new business, one son who might become a world-class boxer, another a physician. In actuality, various family members struggled with learning English, with earning a living, with financial difficulty, with assimilation, with memories, with medical problems, with frustration at not being able to accomplish what they wished to, with deferral of citizenship, and difficulties with the law.[26] Furthermore, there was conflict within the family. The parents divorced, and each left the United States.

None of these experiences are unique to the Tsarnaevs, and none fully justify, or even explain, why the brothers would engage in terrorism. Still, we ignore these factors at our peril.

INTERGENERATIONAL TRANSMISSION OF TRAUMA

One of the most difficult things for the people of Cambridge and Boston to grasp or understand is why Dzhokhar, especially, could engage in terrorism that may have any shades of anti-American motivation. What they missed is that, while Dzhokhar had a pretty much American life from age 9 or so onward, neither his past, nor the past of his ancestors, was washed away by that American experience. They saw no past; therefore they assumed, wrongly, that it was irrelevant. They missed the possibility that his family's past, even those aspects of it that occurred before he was born, was likely to affect him.

The friends' argument goes, he was just one of us. He had no exposure to trauma here in the United States, and certainly did not discuss any experiences that would lead us to believe he was suffering from post-traumatic stress. He was, they felt, as American, and as safe, as the next student at CRLS (many of whom are immigrants from one or another place). And he seemed so "chill," sweet, and nice. He was so helpful to his friends when they were in need. But they all missed some essential part of their friend, some essential identity, or emotion, or psychic reality. Either that or he is innocent. Either that or he was framed. Either that or his brother brainwashed him. But what if he is guilty, not framed, and not brainwashed? How are we to possibly understand why he would be angry enough, mean-spirited enough, violent enough to kill and maim random people—children, adults, elderly? What could possibly make him vulnerable to becoming a bomber?

While Dzhokhar may not have experienced trauma in Cambridge, he almost certainly did in Kyrgyzstan, when his father was imprisoned and beaten. Besides that, however, there is other trauma he may have carried, for people carry not only their own past, but the past of their ancestors, in their lives. Let's take a look at the timeline in Chapter 1. The very beginning of the timeline is in the year 1095, the launching of the first Crusade—where Christians, inspired by Pope Urban, went on the first of several expeditions with the goal of defeating Islam. The messy and complicated politics inspiring this are known to historians but beyond the scope of this book. Suffice it to say that this moment seems to be reverberating over 1,000 years later, with Muslims feeling persecuted by Christians and other non-Muslims, waging asymmetrical warfare in the form of terrorism. Did the Tsarnaevs experience bias, stereotyping, prejudice, or unfair treatment because of being Muslim? Maybe or maybe not, but whether or not they did directly, there is little doubt that they knew that there was widespread prejudice in the United States. Keep in mind that they arrived in the United States in 2002, when Americans were expressing a very high degree of hatred against Muslims. They were here for the several years during which the long-term effects of September 11 were felt—including deprivation of freedoms for everyone, and targeting of Muslim young men by law enforcement, including the FBI. Cambridge, Massachusetts, probably has less anti-Muslim bias than most cities. But we live in a global community. And throughout the United States, Muslims were treated with suspicion and hatred, often being told to go "home," meaning to leave the United States (even though to some of them, the United States was home) often being beaten, often being called "terrorist."

That is a quick summary of the big picture. But the intergenerational transmission of trauma is also personal. For the Tsarnaevs, a key date is 1944, when Stalin decided to simply wipe the country of Chechnya out of existence. All Chechens, about 400,000 people, were deported, in horrendous conditions, often having to travel hundreds of miles by train, many dying along the way, some being shot by soldiers. Estimates vary, but it seems that 30–50 percent of them died within the first year.[27] These numbers make this comparable to the Middle Passage of African American history or to the genocide of Cambodians by the Khmer Rouge or to the genocide of Jewish people in Europe by the Nazis. Indeed, perhaps Stalin found, in Hitler, a role model for these actions.

But none of Tamerlan and Dzhokhar's family who came to the United States had been born by 1944. And none of today's African Americans made the Middle Passage. And few of the Jewish people in the United States today are actual survivors of the Holocaust. So why, then, might they bear the scars of something they never experienced in person? This is where we must draw on researchers and clinicians who have noted serious and troubling effects, across generations, of extreme trauma. Researchers are just now learning the very specific biological, psychological, and social elements of the transmission of trauma. Let's look at some possibilities. It is not surprising that people who experience extreme trauma do not want to talk about it. Avoidance is a normal reaction to trauma. Yet, researchers and clinicians have also learned that it does not help—indeed, attempts to forget may make the event all the more salient as a determiner of one's life. Think of the person who may have had an automobile accident at a particular intersection. Perhaps the person or someone else was injured in that accident. For those involved, it is hard to pass that intersection without becoming apprehensive. They feel a sense of dread when approaching it. Soon they find a way to avoid that intersection. But the children of those people sense some apprehension or anxiety. They "know" that there is something dangerous about that intersection. They find it a very unfriendly location, and all this may happen without a word being exchanged, and without the child having had any adverse experience connected with the intersection in question. Apply that to fear of dogs. Why is it that some kids who have never had a bad encounter of any kind with a dog may be hysterically afraid when they see even a small puppy coming down the street? Imagine a child whose parent tenses up every time a dog is in the vicinity, who steers clear of all dogs. Imagine this happening dozens of times. Now the child has become sensitized to dogs, without ever having encountered one. In the same fashion, a child whose parent, or grandparent, has been tortured or traumatized may experience apprehension or anxiety when any reminders of the situation of torture come up, even having no knowledge of the reason why.

Now let us take this to another level. Perhaps children have never experienced racism. Their parents, however, being responsible and caring, want to protect them from having to create a response, on the spot, when being the object of racial epithets. Or perhaps their parents want to train them in how to respond to authorities so that they do not get themselves into deep trouble. In the United States, this may take the form of young black males being socialized by parents in how to act when being stopped and frisked. In Palestine, it may take the form of Palestinian elders teaching young men how to act in the presence of Israeli soldiers, or how to act when in an Israeli prison. In these cases, the parents must teach children about dangers even before they experience dangers, and here the benefit of protection outweighs the risk of scaring the child unnecessarily. This is another example of intergenerational transmission of trauma.

But perhaps the most common situation of intergenerational transmission of trauma, worldwide, and the most likely implicated in the case of the accused Boston Marathon bombers, is the situation where parents bear the scars of abuse, trauma, and/or torture at the hands of either a known or unknown other, and where the children learn about it either by witnessing or being told about it. Even though the children have not been harmed, they may also not be able to fully discuss the depth of fear and concern they have for parents who, using all their energy to recover and resume a life of safety, are unwilling or unable, or think it unwise, to talk about their experiences with the next generation. In addition, the children may not want to burden their parents further by asking about the experience. Following the trauma or abuse, the family may make significant changes—for example, someone leaves, or the family escapes, at night. These changes inevitably include multiple losses, which also are often not discussed.

In the case of the Tsarnaev brothers, the family trauma started at least as far back as 1944, when their father's father was part of the forced migration from Chechnya. In this migration, the loss was enormous—30–50 percent of the migrants died. The Tsarnaev brothers' grandfather was one of the lucky survivors of the trip to what is now Kyrgyzstan. Once there, surviving families set about making efforts to continue to survive, getting work as they could, getting food as they could, and solving problems as they could. Perhaps the Tsarnaev brothers' grandfather had some skills or luck, or both, because he was able to survive well enough that their father could attend college and study law. But survival and even thriving is not grounds for forgetting, or for the next generation, or the one after that, to forget.

Complicating all this is the fact that, for hundreds of years, Chechens have been considered to be, and have been proud to be, strong, resilient, and not at all easily intimidated. Indeed, it seems to have become a kind of responsibility of Chechens to uphold this reputation. In order to do so, some of the knowledge of what can happen if one lets down one's guard must be transferred down through the generations. In addition to that, in Chechnya, as in many parts of the world, family feuds are passed down through generations. It is, then, important for their safety and survival, for one's offspring to know that there is a feud, that one must keep this in mind when interacting with the other family, and that there is danger inherent in the relationships.

ADOLESCENT NEUROLOGICAL DEVELOPMENT AND JUDGMENT

Over the past 15 or so years, neuroscientists and experts in adolescence have been examining evidence that, during adolescence and into early adulthood (up to about age 25 or so), immature brain development leads to poorer decision making, and greater amenability to influence or coercion by others.[28] Determining whether these factors should be considered at his trial is beyond the scope of this book. But for the purposes of understanding the many complex, interacting factors that converged in a fateful decision on the part of Dzhokhar, it is useful to consider his age, and the likely developmental processes that may have played a role.

> What rational and psychological skills do adolescents and young adults bring to the decision of whether to engage in a terrorist act? The answer is an incompletely developed decision-making apparatus that will not be complete till age 25 or so. Psychologists believe that the human brain is not prepared to assess and make decisions about the risks and threats of the modern world. Add to this the challenges of making such decisions with an apparatus that affords adolescents a solid ability to analyze pros and cons, but a very strong bias toward pros, toward near term rewards, and toward risk-taking. The bias toward risk-taking may be a result of not yet having developed intuitive or gist reactions to events—the kind of quick analysis that Gladwell was talking about in the popular book *Blink*.[29] (Explanation in Baird, et al., *The Teen Brain*)[30]

Adults might have a stronger emotional intuitive negative reaction toward engaging in terrorist activity. (Is it a good idea to blow yourself up in order to blow others up? . . . Most adults are likely to have a strong reaction that leads them to avoid such a choice.) Indeed, in some situations, adult risk analysis may be weighted a little too heavily on avoidance of low incidence, disastrous outcomes as a result of this gist thinking . . . adolescents do not yet have this gist capacity well-developed. As you will see, in some instances, this may even give adolescents an advantage in decision-making, but it sometimes disadvantages them. Furthermore, adolescents are biased against looking at long-term eventualities . . . their minds simply do not process future risk well, and they tend to choose near-term gain or pleasure, even if it comes with long-term risk, more so than adults. Some risks may be less worrisome than others. Getting a radical haircut or risking a small amount of money, for example, or choosing to play football, while not without serious potential consequence, are risks we more or less accept as normal for adolescents. Even driving a bit fast or trying out a motorcycle. These are things we know bring some risks, but a degree of risk that most parents accept, even if reluctantly, are not unusual parts of growing up.[31]

But for youth deciding to engage in terrorist activities, likely encouraged or even challenged by radical and persuasive speakers who have agendas that do not include the future of the youth, there is grave, unacknowledged risk. These persuasive recruiters can convince young people that performing terrorist acts will be meaningful, and play on their tendency to downplay the future risk by reframing it from the risk of death to opportunity for martyrdom, and from the end of life to the beginning of a heavenly afterlife with Allah. Youth like the Tsarnaevs, who are inclined toward ambition for the future, who want to make a mark on the world, but whose plans to do so seem frustrated, are the perfect victims for such persuasive speakers.

So there is the deadly mix: a young adult trying to figure out his or her identity, who longs for some greatness, some way to contribute to the world. His or her hopes to be a physician, engineer, dentist, attorney, do not seem to be working out, yet he or she still has to figure out who he or she is and how to make his or her mark in the world: a preacher, an ideology, an identity, and a way to make a meaningful life. For some youth, this seems an irresistible offer. Dzhokhar seems to have been one of those youth.

WAS DZHOKHAR DEPRESSED?

A commonsense explanation for why some people might be willing to give up on nonviolent actions as a force for political change, and engage in violence that is sure to limit their own life, is that they may be depressed and/or self-destructive. It seems very likely that Dzhokhar and Tamerlan both knew that the actions they are alleged to have engaged in would end their lives as they knew them, leading to either death or a life incarcerated. In that sense they may be seen to have been self-destructive, even if their motives were, in their eyes and in the eyes of some others, altruistic.

What is the evidence that Dzhokhar may have been clinically depressed? When diagnosing depression, mental health professionals consider both general outlook and specific symptoms. In terms of general outlook, a mental health professional would want to know whether the person had hopes for the future, whether there was recent loss, whether depression runs in the family, whether the individual has social, emotional, and practical support from family and/or friends. Specific symptoms include difficulties with sleep or eating, persistent deep sadness, lack of energy, irritability, lack of social support, difficulty concentrating, low self-esteem, feelings of guilt, thoughts of death. On some of these counts, Dzhokhar would be seen to be at some risk of depression, and at more serious risk of dysthymia, a kind of less intense, but long-lasting depression. In addition, heavy use of marijuana is associated with depression that is independent of, not caused by, marijuana. In other words, many heavy marijuana users are depressed for other reasons. We cannot conclude based on the heavy marijuana use discussed earlier that Dzhokhar was depressed, but it is another factor that should make us wonder.[32]

Dzhokhar's hopes for the future had undergone several instances of downsizing, in spite of quite considerable evidence that he was intelligent, academically successful, well rounded, and had good enough social skills to manage a career in his chosen field of engineering. Yet over the period of time from when he arrived at college until the Marathon bombings, he changed plans twice, his grades plummeted, he seems to have stopped doing schoolwork, indicated to a friend that he was no longer interested in academics, and found himself in a great deal of college debt. It seems he was on his own to finance college, at an age and in a situation where each of his family members had concerns of their own, and their ability to help or guide him was reduced. Add to that the image he had among friends of being relaxed, the fact that he was no longer in the supportive environment of his hometown, and the stage is set for his hopes for the future to be compromised. As for recent loss, Dzhokhar had lost the environment he had grown up in, where he had seemed to do well. He lost the presence of his parents, who had both moved thousands of miles away. He may well have seen it as likely that his dad would die soon, since his father's stated reason for moving back to Dagestan was that if he was going to die he would want to die there. He lost the hope of visiting his father, because his passport did not come through in time for a summer visit. He had a more subtle loss in that the relationship he had had with his brother in the past was now changed because his brother, having become devout and demanding the same of others, expected more religious behavior from Dzhokhar. Furthermore, it seems safe to assume that, when Tamerlan returned from Dagestan, he had changed.

During this same time, Tamerlan's family took some financial hits, including the loss of the subsidy that had enabled them to stay in the apartment where Dzhokhar grew up.

As to whether depression runs in the Tsarnaev family, that is not known. It seems likely that Dzhokhar's father may have suffered from depression and traumatic stress after losing his job, being imprisoned, and being beaten in Kyrgyzstan, where he had held a good job. In addition, coming to the United States and not really succeeding here must have been demoralizing. None of these add up to the sort of depression that is likely to be inherited, however, so we do not know.

As for specific symptoms, we know from his tweets that Dzhokhar had difficulty with sleep. We do not have much reason to think he was more than occasionally irritable. There is an association between depression and heavy marijuana use, but the association is not so strong as to enable us to say that if he was using a lot of marijuana he was likely to be depressed.

Overall, then, it seems that depression may have been one factor among many contributing to the decisions that led Dzhokhar to be accused of the Boston Marathon bombing.

4

❖

Who Benefits When Kids Are Recruited to Violence?[1]

Obviously only a small minority of youth are successfully recruited to lives immersed in violence. Another small group is kidnaped, coerced, tricked, or otherwise forced into it. Although most youth manage to avoid or resist, or be protected by others from violence, I have never seen an instance of a young person living a life of violence—either as perpetrator or victim, or both—where no adult was benefiting from it. Recruiters are savvy enough to recognize kids who are at risk of recruitment. They are kids whose families are not vigilant, or are not present. Kids who have suffered previous trauma, perhaps, and who are lost in some way. Kids who are frightened or depressed are also frequently targeted by adults who see them as likely recruits. Kids who need someone in their court, who need to be special, where specialness substitutes for love. They are similar to kids who are identified by sexual perpetrators and recruited as victims. And recruiters and perpetrators similarly have some uncanny ability to sense kids at risk—a kind of vulnerable kid radar. That is not to imply that they have any care, love, empathy, or concern for such kids. Rather, they are more likely to see the kids as objects to use in the interest of gaining money, power, or fame, or some combination of those, with no awareness or concern over the cost to the kids.

In many cases, the adults benefiting the most when kids are immersed in violence are far enough removed from the victim or perpetrator to appear separate, innocent, upstanding, and respectable. In other cases, the adults are clearly connected, engaged, and immediate beneficiaries of the services provided by the youth. A 13-year-old who is selling drugs, bringing them from the supplier to the customer, may see himself as well compensated. Perhaps he has access to a weapon, and finds himself respected and feared in the neighborhood. Maybe his power attracts girls to him. He may feel that he is benefiting greatly from this opportunity. But the person who is supplying the drugs, and who recruited him, is gaining a lot more money, and with it a lot more prestige, and less exposure to the outside world. And the person who supplied it in bulk to the immediate supplier may have a clandestine organization where he gets the drugs from someone at the docks and brings them to the suppliers, getting compensated with a percentage of the value of the drugs at each step of the operation. And behind him is someone who finances the operation and who never sees or touches drugs, or drug runners, or customers, and may in fact be thousands of miles away. He or she may be making a fair amount of money from this operation, allowing him or her to live a very luxurious life, which his or her neighbors attribute to success in some mainstream business. But consider this question: Who, among all these people, is most likely to be arrested, or shot, or roughed up?

Sociologists tell us that the alternate economy, including the wealth generated by the business of dealing in illicit drugs, is about as large as the legal, mainstream economy. Keep in mind, as well, that the two economies are hardly separate. The money earned by the every person in the chain described earlier is likely to be spent in the mainstream economy, buying items from clothes and jewelry to cars and houses. Some of the benefits that some adults receive when kids are engaged in violence are not monetary, but power benefits. The benefits may be measured in power, or loyalty, or love.

What does this have to do with good kids and terrorism? When youth are recruited to terrorism, their lives are bound to become immersed in violence, as they become victims and perpetrators of violence, and their lives will very likely shortly be over. Who benefits then? Their recruiter benefits in nonmonetary terms, by reputation, power, and respect. Furthermore, the recruiter's organization's leaders, often far from the action, also benefit by gaining power and respect, and with each victory, gaining more financial support from ex-pats who are financing the rebellion or separatist movement, or efforts at regime-change. Furthermore, in a twist of fate that is not always obvious, the organization's enemies also gain; when they have an enemy, they can use the existence of the enemy to create fear and then to build trust, patriotism, and loyalty. In this way, the militia leaders gain when the children they kidnap or recruit are success-ful in bombing a civilian location, but so are the government officials, as the fear generated by the terrorist actions leads to further trust, loyalty, and patriotism and even provides them opportunities to play out their leadership role, by committing to rid the country of the blight of terror-ism, for example.

Thus the tasks of the Islamist recruiters are parallel to recruiters in North, South or Latin America, the European Union, Asia, or Africa: identify vulnerable kids, sort them into those who will be good as part of the team and those who will benefit the cause more by acting alone—or who are too high a risk to have as part of the group, and can be encouraged to act alone. After identifying and sorting, with promises of intangible rewards, the recruiters encourage the ones who will not be part of the group—in the case of the Islamist recruiters, these promises may be bene-fits in an afterlife, such as having a special place as a martyr, getting lots of virgins, assuring their families and friends will go to heaven. Once they are recruited, recruiters can use them to do mischief or worse. The recruiters will probably never hear directly from those youth again. The youth will either be dead or discovered and imprisoned. The possibilities for these young people for leading a productive life as part of civil society are very likely over. The devastation for them, their loved ones, and, if they carry off their attack, their communities, has just begun. Promises of virgins and martyrdom and heaven for their kin seem very far removed indeed from the hell that relatives, neighbors, friends, and acquaintances of the young terrorists go through on earth as a result of the success of the recruiters.

The following are composite sketches drawn from my experience work-ing with youth engaged in violence. They illustrate the general point that kids all over the world are recruited to violence and that somewhere, some adult or adults stand to gain. The goal of these sketches and the commen-tary that follow is to put terrorism by young recruits into the context of a worldwide problem: youth being used by adults to benefit themselves at the cost of the youth. Later in this chapter, all these instances are put in the context of child labor. That is, when an adolescent or young adult is recruited to engage in violence, he or she is being recruited to something very much like what are known internationally as the "worst forms of child labor."

SARASI

"Her mother burned," the small Tamil girl said, speaking into my ear, in a too-loud whisper. It was a balmy morning, the start of another 100-degree

Sri Lankan day. "In a camp," she continued, pointing at Sarasi, a beautiful child whose dark eyes were strong, determined, and distant. Deaths were agonizingly common in the lives of children born during the 26-year civil war, but life and death in one of the dreaded camps for Internally Displaced Persons (IDP), especially a death by fire, was worthy of notice. Sarasi picked up the story, as if reciting into the air. "My mother was cooking when her clothes caught fire. I was down the road getting water. I heard her screams, but others got there before me." She paused. "Later, she died." The camp where Sarasi's mother burned was an IDP camp for ethnic Tamils displaced in the war[2] that pitted them, a separatist minority, against the Sinhalese-dominated government.

Sarasi's father had also died before her eyes, having been shot outside their home. She reports: "The soldiers came to the door and asked for him. When I said he was not home, they pushed me down. My mother told them the baby was asleep in a room, but they broke down the door, found and hit him, then dragged him outside. They made him kneel and then they shot him." After killing her father, the soldiers captured Sarasi's older brother. She remembers how roughly they grabbed him, and that on the next day, a storm washed away the dark trail of his blood. After that, Sarasi had tried to help her mother, who was in shock. Neighbors buried her father because her mother was too weak to do so. Sarasi attended the burial, reciting a familiar prayer at the graveside.

Sarasi was 11 years old when she witnessed her mother's death in the camp. After that, she joined the militant separatist fighting force, the Liberation Tigers of Tamil Eelam—the LTTE. "Joined" implies volunteering, but Sarasi had few choices: the LTTE gave her a means to survive, a mission, and a way to understand the deaths of her parents.

Their deaths, the LTTE claimed, were the result of the Tamil minority being oppressed by the Sinhalese, who were able to kidnap and murder them at will. Her mother's death may have been accidental, but it was an accident that wouldn't have happened if there were no camps—if people weren't displaced by a long, gruesome war. Had the Sri Lankan government treated the Tamils fairly, they would not have had to fight for land and sovereignty. For Sarasi, the LTTE was a family, meeting her basic needs and giving her instructions on how to fight back.

Sarasi, coached by older girl soldiers, focused on becoming a good fighter. She suppressed her feelings and concentrated on building up her strength. She was a proud member of the LTTE. She learned how to clean, assemble, and use an AK-47, and was chosen to be one of the Black Tigers—the elite group deployed on missions where they would intentionally die in the service of killing others. She was glad to make such a strong impact as a Black Tiger, as she would be remembered and honored, forever.

But Sarasi was not to have the opportunity to avenge her parents' deaths, as she was rescued, against her will, by an aid organization. She now lives with her uncle, and attends school. She tried to return twice to the LTTE, but they would not accept "rescued" children. She is resigned to living with her uncle and studying to become a lawyer, in the hope of helping her people. But now, at age 17, she realizes the harsh reality that, as a Tamil in Sri Lanka, she is unlikely to reach that goal. Now that the war is over, it is hard to find the LTTE. Should it rise up again, Sarasi will try to rejoin.

JOSEPHA

Eight thousand miles away, in a depressed Massachusetts city, another beautiful 11-year-old child with straight teeth, dark skin, and hazel eyes watched her father die in front of their home in a melee that included the local police. Years later, her probation officer noted, "She was young and didn't understand much except that her father was bleeding." Josepha, looking at the floor, added, "I wanted to help him, but a police lady held me back." Josepha had come to the attention of the court when she punched another child and gave him a black eye. "He kept asking me questions about my father and what he looked like when he died," she said. "He wouldn't stop, so I hit him," she said, to no one in particular. At that time, her mother was given a referral for Josepha to see a counselor, but, being ill, she was unable to bring Josepha to her appointment, and no one else stepped in to help.

Four years after her father died, Josepha's mother was diagnosed with AIDS. Since medication cocktails were not then available, she was dying, losing weight and control of her body. Her grandmother, who speaks no English and spends most of her time in prayer, was unable to fathom much about Josepha's American life but advised her to pray and be strong. Josepha's older brother tried to support the family with money "earned" as a lookout for local drug dealers, but he was caught and violated his probation while trying to find illegal ways to get money for his family. He was placed in juvenile detention. One of her uncles is also in jail. "I don't know why," Josepha says, answering a question no one had asked.

Josepha's teachers were in disbelief when she said she was late for school because she had to help her dying mother. "They said my mother needed nurses and that she wanted me to study, but I couldn't leave her until she ate something in the morning. She only ate if I gave her food. So I had to stop going to school." One day, suspended from school, when she was hanging out at her cousin's house, Josepha met a young man, a member of the gang that protects her block. "He was cute and had a lot of ideas. He told me he liked me." She liked him, too. As they talked, he said he knew her father was "a man with heart," and that his death was not an accident—he had been killed by the police, who were called by a rival gang member. The police, he said, shot the first Latino male they saw on the block, and then covered it up when they found out it was the wrong man. He said members of the other gang "snitched" on her brother. "If it weren't for them, my brother would be here right now, not in detention. In detention, he is not himself. He is empty; his eyes are dead."

After meeting the young man, Josepha wanted to join the gang. She went with him to his home, his grandfather's house. The defeated old man had long since stopped trying to correct his grandson, who had, in his eyes, become too American, but he still called out a greeting from out of sight when they went up the stairs to the young man's room. He told her to relax and take off her shoes, then he talked her into getting undressed so he could see if she was strong enough, and he raped her. He said that he only did this with girls who were strong, and that, once she was used to it, she would like it. He told her some other boys would help to give her practice.

Josepha did not call it rape. She felt it was a test to see if she could be part of the gang, so she endured the pain even though it was worse than anything she had ever experienced. Before leaving her that day, the young man let her hold his knife and, warning her not to tell anyone what he was doing because it was against the rules, he let her hold his gun. She thought it was a sign that she had shown strength. He also gave her a cell phone, saying he would call the next day. But by the next morning, he was in a coma. "The other gang sent two guys to find him and they crushed his skull with a rock," she explained, still looking down.

Josepha became more determined than ever. She lifted weights and avoided the police who, she believed, were as much the enemy as the rival gang. She waited for news about her friend. She felt strong, she said, unconvincingly. "I talk to my father, even though I cannot see him, and he gives me strength, because he is with God." Josepha's cousin introduced her to other gang members, and Josepha continued strengthening herself. Two days before her initiation, when she would have to withstand being kicked and punched, Josepha was brought into court by her grandmother after a Spanish-speaking police officer said that Josepha was in trouble again, this time for not attending school. Josepha did not speak during her hearing. She only looked down when asked to respond. The

probation officer had heard that Josepha was about to join the gang officially. He talked to her grandmother, who agreed to send Josepha to live
with relatives in a different town where Josepha was required, under the
terms of probation, to attend school. She was uneasy, but her aunt and
uncle cajoled her by saying if she did well in school, they would give her
a new cell phone. Then, she told herself, she would go back and join
the gang. She liked schoolwork, but feared the kids in the new school.
"They don't like me. They want to beat me up, but are afraid of me." And
they were; they had seen her knife. Her teachers wanted Josepha, now a
junior, to attend college. They thought that she could get a scholarship.
But Josepha dismissed such ideas; she could not imagine herself in college.
That, she thought, was for other girls.

SUDAN

The stories of Josepha and Sarasi—8,000 miles apart, yet eerily similar—
reflect the vulnerability of children immersed in violence—especially if
they are separated from their families, or their families were killed violently. The horrors of the Armenian and Cambodian genocides and the
Holocaust continue to reverberate for the children and grandchildren
who survived. There is little doubt the ongoing genocide in Sudan today
will affect the survivors, even those fortunate enough to become refugees
in safe countries. Some children are remarkably resilient, but violence
changes them, and programs designed to undo these changes cannot
reach all who need them, nor are they uniformly effective for all.

In countries like Sudan, the future is dim for so many children, especially those of the Dinka tribe. To them, being a child soldier may be more
appealing than the alternatives, such as slavery. Humanitarian agencies in
Sudan attempt to disarm, demobilize, and reintegrate child soldiers, but
they have limits to their services, especially with regard to funding.

> I joined the SPLA (Sudan Peoples' Liberation Army) when I was 13.
> I am from Bahr Al Ghazal. They demobilized me in 2001 and took
> me to Rumbek, but I was given no demobilization documents. Now,
> I am stuck here because my family was killed in a government attack
> and because the SPLA would re-recruit me. At times I wonder why
> I am not going back to SPLA, half of my friends have and they seem
> to be better off than me.[3]

"In the Sudanese context," says Sudan expert Randall Fegley, "distinc-
tions between slaves, child soldiers, and street children are fluid rather

than mutually exclusive."[4] Street children are easily recruited as child soldiers. Child soldiers, after being demobilized, usually are without a surviving family and a source of income, leaving them few choices for supporting themselves. They are vulnerable to being sold as slaves or prostitutes, to living on the streets, or to returning to the militia. In many cases, the communities and their own families fear them and do not want them to return. The United Nations and other agencies attempting to help former child soldiers may have the opportunity to work with a village or community, to prepare it for the reintegration of the children. But in Sudan, which has many war-torn areas, those communities may not have survived.

> Locals in the SPLA stronghold of Rumbek complain that many of the former child soldiers are unable to adjust to civilian life. Too traumatised by war and prone to picking fights if they do not have their own way, they are viewed as troublemakers.[5]

Merciless raids on villages in the south, where the most villagers died, left thousands of children orphaned and homeless. A large number of boys, many of whom were tending animals remotely when their villages were attacked, gathered over the course of a year or more and walked, together, hundreds of miles across deserts to reach the refugee camps. Many died on the journey. A few thousand survivors, known as the "Lost Boys of Sudan," were given asylum in the United States. Their stirring stories are readily available on the Internet, in books, and in films.[6] Many are tireless advocates for the peers they left behind. In 2011, South Sudan gained independence, but fighting between factions began in 2013.

YOUTH AND VIOLENCE: WHO STANDS TO GAIN?

Youth like Sarasi and Josepha garner the public's attention when they become or threaten to become perpetrators of violence, but we seldom hear the rest of the story—the violence they have experienced and witnessed that leads them to accept it as normal. For Sarasi, Josepha, and millions of others—kids on every continent, in wealthy and poor countries—violence permeates their lives. They have been victims many times over and are poised to do the only thing that makes sense to them: use violence to solve problems. Unless they are luckier than others, they lack role models to guide them—people who could mentor them, lighting a path that leads to a better life.

Most adults respond to youths who commit violent acts according to their own preconceptions. Some say that a violent child is bad to the core, and demand that such a child be kept away from society. There is a growing trend in the United States toward trying and sentencing youthful offenders as adults, sending them to adult prisons, even sentencing children to life in prison without parole. Once they are in adult prison, children are subject to repeated sexual assault by adult inmates; the prison security system doesn't protect them. In May 2010, the U.S. Supreme Court heard a case involving a young man who was 13 years old and mentally disabled when sentenced to life in prison without parole for alleged sexual assault. The Court decided that life in prison without parole would not be allowed for crimes short of homicide, committed by youth under age 18.[7] "The United States . . . [was] the only country in the world where a thirteen year old is known to be sentenced to life in prison without the possibility of parole."[8] Still many adults argue that if a child commits a crime, he or she should be punished as an adult. Having little hope of a child's ability to change, they do not favor rehabilitation.

Those who do favor rehabilitation prefer counseling, family support, alternative schools, and comprehensive service packages sometimes called "wraparound" services, that include a variety of community, educational, and mental health supports. Multi-systemic therapy, or MST is an approach with the best-documented and researched effectiveness. MST therapists work with youth at risk of immediate detention and with their caregivers. Their success is measured by reduced recidivism. By that measure, MST does well.[9]

Recent advances in neuroscience support the view that children should not be held accountable in a manner identical to adults. It is understood now that brain development is not complete until the mid-20s. Adolescents are less capable of complex decision making or self-control. Laurence Steinberg and Elizabeth S. Scott, a psychologist and an attorney, respectively, with expertise in adolescent development, use the phrase, "less guilty" to describe adolescent responsibility for criminal acts.[10] Psychologists, attorneys, and judges are hampered by a lack of data to form valid determinations about which adolescents might be rehabilitated and which practices, interventions, and treatments are best. For those who cannot now be rehabilitated, and who must be separated from others, society should ask what makes better sense for such separation, an adult prison or a safer setting with constructive activity, in the hope that, one day, more adequate means of rehabilitation might be developed.

PREVENTION

Adults who favor rehabilitation and prevention are asking what can be done in communities and families to ensure that children do not become violent. How can they be nurtured early in life? How can parents become more involved with their children? Those who value rehabilitation and prevention may launch programs that focus on strengthening the family bond. Some programs attempt to strengthen, or rebuild, entire communities to provide healthier environments, for example, the Harlem Children's Zone.[11]

Although the views of those who favor prevention and rehabilitation appear to be opposite of those who favor adult-style punishment and confinement, they both focus on the child as the one to be helped or changed. Both viewpoints assume that the core problem is the child (or perhaps the family or community) and that intervention should help the child become strong enough to resist peer and other forms of pressure. For decades, such views have been a major focus in attempts to reduce youth violence.

FUNDAMENTAL ATTRIBUTION ERROR

Perhaps this focus on the child can be explained by the social psychology concept, "fundamental attribution error." Psychologists describe a well-documented bias, especially on the part of Americans and others from Western countries, to attribute unacceptable actions to internal character deficits or dispositions. Thus, when a child is carrying a weapon or engaging in violence or terrorist actions, the question generally asked is, "What is wrong with this child?" The assumption is that the answer will reflect an internal problem—mental illness, perhaps, or inadequate parenting, or inherited vulnerability—the answer will be found by "zooming in" on the child, focusing efforts on changing the child's behavior or locking up the child.

This bias to see unacceptable actions as reflecting personality, psychopathology, or character leads to ignoring situational factors and pressures. Without considering the horrors experienced by Sarasi and Josepha, for example, we might see them as mentally ill, or having a genetic predisposition to violence, or possessing a neurological problem that manifests in aggressive, antisocial tendencies, and so on. Even when we know about the afflictions they've suffered, we might imagine that such miseries caused them to become mentally ill—perhaps with posttraumatic stress disorder (PTSD), which can result in violence. This perspective has considerable acceptance among progressive mental health and human service workers. However, even this enlightened perspective fails to consider that children such as Josepha and Sarasi experience violence as a normal part of life. From their viewpoints, violence is normal not because the media promotes it, but because they have actually experienced it. As its victims and witnesses, they see violence being perpetrated by the authorities as well as by gang members. It is qualitatively different to have lived with violence as a normal aspect of life, especially through a young life, as compared to having had an ordinary life, and then experiencing trauma as an aberration—whether that trauma is part of war or in peacetime.

VULNERABILITY TO RECRUITMENT

To justify the tendency to see deficits in a child, Americans sometimes point out exceptional victimized adolescents and adults, who have resisted violence despite strong pressures to succumb to it. These individuals are, no doubt, exemplary and their resistance laudable. Some say that their ability to resist is proof that it is not the violence in life that causes children to engage in violence, but rather a personal vulnerability in their genetic or constitutional makeup. The temperamental or constitutional strength, experience, or circumstances that enable some children to resist pressures should be studied and replicated, if possible, while taking into account that resistance is sometimes risky, since it could cause the child to become a target of would-be recruiters. Resistance can also be futile because the recruiters could kidnap and threaten children with death themselves or the deaths of their family members, thereby forcing them to join the militia in spite of their protests. Therefore the child who succumbs to threats may have made a decision for the sake of survival—his or her own or others'.

To expect children living in a world of violence to resist or avoid being kidnapped, conscripted, or seduced through the power of their own will is wishful thinking. The life experiences of Josepha, Sarasi, and literally millions of other children render them helpless to solving their problems and making their lives meaningful. It is the defenselessness of the youth that enables adults who stand to gain (money, power, or both) to recruit them to violence. Few adults focus on the moral, emotional, or psychological deficits of the recruiters, or those who reward the recruiters—typically adults, sometimes mainstream. Perhaps more important, rarely do adults focus on reducing violence by reducing, much less eliminating, the economic benefits or power of those who stand to gain.

By looking only at a child's flaws, whether inborn or the result of misfortune, we miss seeing that it is adults who profit from the child's vulnerability. But rarely are these adults held to account for the actions of the children they've recruited. Therefore, they can maintain the status quo.

A NEW FOCUS ON THOSE WHO BENEFIT

Recently, new discussions on how to prevent violence to and by youth have been initiated throughout the world. Many have centered on children employed in jobs that put them at risk. The International Labor

Organization has taken a visible role in encouraging the world to prohibit the "worst forms of child labor."[12] Both the U.S. Senate and the U.S. House of Representatives have considered bills that would hold businesses responsible for their suppliers, even those outside the United States, to adhere to fair and decent labor practices, including not having children work in unsuitable jobs and for long periods of time. Organizations have sprung up to encourage businesses to avoid dealing with those that engage in the worst forms of child labor, and to encourage consumers to boycott such businesses. In a timely example, the Basel Action Network has begun certifying companies that engage in safe practices in recycling e-waste.[13] Businesses are being encouraged not to send electronic waste such as old computers, cell phones, and so on, to unscrupulous recyclers who knowingly engage in practices that harm children and adults. Such unscrupulous companies send discarded electronics to villages in less-developed countries, where lack of the resources to protect workers and others causes illness among the children and adults engaged in the recycling work, and even among the citizens of those communities.[14] Early in 2010, the UN Special Representative to the secretary-general on business and human rights, John Ruggie, established a website dealing with the "Corporate Responsibility to Respect Human Rights."[15]

With regard to child soldiers, Aryeh Neier, president of the Open Society Institute, suggested in 2005 "international agreements," "shaming lists," and "so-called smart sanctions, such as travel bans on leaders of governments employing child soldiers, or freezes on their assets abroad . . ." as a means to reduce the attractiveness of recruiting child soldiers.[16] The first case to be heard by the International Criminal Court is that of Thomas Lubanga, a Congolese accused of recruiting child soldiers. Lubanga is charged with seizing children even as young as 10 years old and having them fight with his militia.[17] Others from the Congo have been charged with similar crimes. Radhika Coomaraswamy, under secretary-general and special representative of the Secretary General of the United Nations for Children and Armed Conflict, says of this process, "The deterrence effect of even one conviction should be substantial."[18] Evidence for the effectiveness of the trial, according to Coomaraswamy, is the high degree of interest in the outcome.[19] It is hoped that Lubanga's trial will put other recruiters on notice that they, too, may face serious legal consequences. No one is naive enough to think that this will eliminate the practice, but it should reduce it.

Given the extent that the recruiters and those who kidnap youth and induce them to engage in violence are benefiting politically and/or economically, the enforcement of existing laws would make such actions unprofitable and risky, thus reducing the incentive and, in turn, reducing youth violence more effectively than one-to-one or small-group interventions. Just as the efforts to reduce profits to companies that deal with unscrupulous suppliers might reduce the number of children engaged in the worst forms of child labor, so if the profits gained from children involved in the illegal drug trade in the United States and elsewhere were to be dramatically curtailed, there would be little incentive to recruit, train, and arm children. With regard to child prostitution, *New York Times* columnist Nicholas Kristof has asserted that those who profit from child trafficking and prostitution might be stopped if interventions aimed at making the business less profitable were undertaken.[20] Kristof and Sheryl WuDunn[21] have brought attention to the economic aspect—the common "brothel business model"[22]—of forced prostitution. They suggest that intervention, including international condemnation, with economic repercussions, can be an effective way to reduce child prostitution.

As for children and firearms in the United States, Geoffrey Canada and Marian Wright Edelman have pointed out that gun manufacturers profit when children have easy access to firearms.[23]

These questions and considerations, and the interventions they suggest, while not expected to eliminate youth violence, hold promise as an efficient way to lessen the number of children kidnapped and coerced into violence, as well as those who might be seduced by the false hope of honor and satisfaction through revenge. Despite the appearance of such good ideas, however, implementation and follow-up have, to date, had limited effectiveness. What is needed is a sense of outrage and effort on the part of concerned citizens. The 2007 U.S. Decent Working Conditions and Fair Competition Act, for example, would have held American corporations responsible for the labor practices of their international suppliers. It died in committee in both the House and Senate, despite a Harris poll showing that a majority of Americans favor such a bill, and despite the fact that it had 26 cosponsors in the Senate and 176 in the House of Representatives.[24] Business interests undoubtedly mounted compelling arguments and/or pressure against the bill. Any action against corporations failing to adhere to safe labor practices again fell to the local action committees as the American Congress decided against taking on such responsibility.

The Basel Action Network reports that about 80 percent of the electronic waste that is collected for "recycling" winds up in "developing countries, where it is processed in primitive conditions."[25] The UN Special Representative to the Secretary General for Business and Human Rights reports, "While many companies state that they respect human rights, the SRSG has found that few companies have systems in place to support such statements."[26] Encouraging lawmakers and business executives to attentively look at their suppliers' actions and workplaces is a simple and straightforward way that people may help to reduce the number of children engaged in unsuitable or dangerous forms of labor.

FINDING THOSE WHO BENEFIT FROM YOUTH VIOLENCE

Sweatshops, farms, brothels, and e-waste sites that employ youth in unsafe or inappropriate activities can be found in every country on earth from Albania to Zimbabwe—including developed countries such as the United States, the United Kingdom, Spain, and the Netherlands. Those who own or manage these places are in violation of Convention 182 of the International Labor Organization, an agency of the UN that prohibits the "Worst Forms of Child Labor,"[27] which is signed by all member countries of the UN. These employers benefit economically from the labor of children engaged in risky work that, in some cases, causes the children to become emotionally or physically disabled, or physically sick. Interventions by the international community, such as active boycotts of the items produced by these employers, have sometimes been effective in stopping the more egregious practices that have characterized their businesses. But without the necessary community support to combat them, these practices have not been eradicated.

It is crucial, although difficult and challenging, to get beyond the more visible employers, such as farms, mines, and sweatshops, to the private, and sometimes hidden, alternative economy employers engaged in ventures—militia, gangs, traffickers, and brothels—that employ youth in work that is, by its very nature, violent. Sometimes these employers remain invisible because of the cooperation of local law enforcement; in those cases, intervention is necessary to make corruption of the police undesirable and unprofitable. There is documentation in social science and law-enforcement literature indicating that throughout the world, many organizations that employ children in dangerous and violent activities are not just haphazard ventures that "happen" to be profitable. Rather, some are well planned, well organized, and thoughtfully executed ventures that depend on the availability of child labor (including lookouts, prostitutes, and soldiers) for their profits. One can look for a trail of money and power, a trail that will, according to sociologists, inevitably and rapidly lead back to the mainstream culture.[28] Ensuring that youth not succumb to a life of violence will affect not only the alternate economy, but will drastically reduce cash flow to those mainstream individuals who have hidden the source of their cash flow, often attributing it to financial acumen or timing.

Around the world, children are seduced by lies into a culture of hideous violence and suffering, where the ultimate beneficiaries can include people living in luxury, in safe communities, and who are presented as model citizens. Recently, a much-applauded U.S. television series, *The Wire*, provided a fictionalized scenario where children were engaged in the selling of drugs within a large, alternate economic venture in which the profits were used in part as campaign contributions to elect public officials who were then reluctant to encourage restrictions that could lead to revealing their own complicity in crime.[29]

The realization that mainstream economies could also be affected if fewer children are engaged in violence may discourage those who might intervene in these alternate economies. As noted earlier, efforts at intervention often fail or fizzle. Therefore, careful planning has to assure that the mainstream economy will be able to offset losses that result from intervention. Youth currently employed in alternate economies, for example, must be able to obtain mainstream job training and jobs that will enable them to contribute to society. There is a parallel here in that successful reintegration of child soldiers also requires gainful employment, so that those former child soldiers will have access to the resources needed to join the law-abiding community.[30] Without the encouragement of job training, such child soldiers are apt to continue lives of violence outside the militia.

In many of the poorest countries, the income gained by children employed in dangerous and violent activities is a necessary contribution to the family. Without that income, family members would not have enough to eat or house themselves. For this reason, caution in the implementation of Convention 182 has proven to be necessary in many settings.

Recent works have brought attention to the complex systems that support the continuation of profitable violence (including violence by and against youth). Psychologist Marc Pilisuk, in *Who Benefits from Global Violence and War*,[31] suggests that networks of wealthy and powerful individuals, mostly male, stand to gain economically from wars and violence around the world. He argues that the accumulation of great wealth and power in the hands of the relatively few who benefit from war leaves society vulnerable to continued and increased conflicts.

In the following section, we consider some of the specific areas where profit from products obtained both legally and illegally contributes to the establishment and/or maintenance of youth violence.

MARKETING FIREARMS, PRISONS, DRUGS, VIRGINS, AND URBAN VIOLENCE CHIC

Profiting from Firearms

Here I was dealing with children dying every day and trying to solve the problem on the streets, and other Americans were sitting in offices designing new and more effective ways to entice children to use handguns.[32]

—Geoffrey Canada

. . . the commanders gave us AK-47 assault rifles and taught us how to dismantle, clean and assemble them. "Hunger will teach you how to shoot," they said.

—Grace Akallo,[33] former child soldier

Foreigners have to reduce the export of weapons to Sri Lanka. Have to stop the weapons.

—Adolescent Interviewee, Sri Lanka, June 2007[34]

When one wants to know who benefits from youth violence, a common place to start with is firearms.[35] While the rights of law-abiding adults to carry firearms continues to be debated, few people would endorse the acquisition of large numbers of illegally acquired firearms carried on the street, on public transportation, and brought into schools, by nonlicensed teenagers. And no one would endorse the practices that lead to eight children being killed each day in the United States. According to the Boston Youth Violence Study's 2006 survey, the majority of youth surveyed, including youth who recently have carried guns, would prefer to live in a world where it was difficult for an adolescent to acquire a gun. Psychological studies have confirmed anecdotal evidence that the mere presence of guns in a given environment increases the level of aggression.[36]

Three considerations have been raised about gun profits in relation to youth. First, there are questions about the efforts to design attractive guns, particularly appealing to the young. Second, the proliferation and widespread use of the Automatic Kalashnikov, or the AK47, a relatively lightweight and easy-to-use automatic weapon that has been supplied to children by adults who have recruited or coerced them into lives of violence of one kind or another. Third, international arms sales by government-endorsed suppliers enrich manufacturers and distributors, bringing tax money into their countries of origin, while devastating war-torn countries, causing death and suffering especially to children and the aged.

Firearms Designed to Be Attractive to Youth

A wide variety of firearms, distinguished only by their designs, can readily be found on the Internet. Some firearms are intentionally designed and styled to appeal to youth and even include a fashion statement. Such products, including pink rifles advertised as "Princess Power,"[37] are easily found online. Many of those may be purchased legally, used legally, and never cause harm to the innocent. Still, every day in the United States, eight children or teenagers are killed by firearms.[38] Beyond the issue of fashion, assault rifles make frequent appearance in popular and rap music in recent years. In fact, there are several artists now known by the name "AK-47."

Lightweight Automatic Rifles: Contributing to the Use of Violence by Children, Including Child Soldiers

The AK-47 rifle is presumed to have enabled young children to fight as child soldiers. Approximately one hundred million AK-47 assault rifles are estimated in use in the world today. Even children as young as six or seven years old can use the weapon. Most weapons as deadly as the AK-47 are too heavy and awkwardly sized for children. Although the AK-47 is not the only lightweight and deadly weapon, it is a widely available and weapon of choice for rebel groups and militia. "They have been glorified in rap music, gangster films and on national flags . . ."[39] The development of the AK-47 in and by itself makes it likely that youth will be recruited for deadly work. The significance of this technology is not only its widespread availability or its relatively lightweight, but that it allows even very young children to shoot hundreds of rounds per minute. In 2006, M. Kalashnikov, developer of the AK-47, said that he was in agreement with UN secretary general Kofi Anan that light weapons are the weapons of mass destruction,[40] and he regretted some of the uses of his invention. Larry Kahaner, author of a book about the AK-47, says the weapon's impact on modern warfare is as strong as the atomic bomb. "Now, the U.S. has the best-disciplined, best-trained soldiers in the world, I believe. But you can put anybody in a Toyota pickup truck, give him an AK-47, and he can go out and give U.S. soldiers a hard time."[41]

On this 90th birthday, Kalashnikov received a great honor when he was named a "Hero of Russia," by Russian president Dmitry Medvedev, in recognition of his development of the AK-47.[42] While there is little doubt that the invention has been a success in its own terms, many former child soldiers, as well as the family members of the victims of child soldiers, find the bestowal of such an honor to be perplexing.

Arms Dealers and Their Home Countries

The selling of international arms is a complex, somewhat secretive business and has indirect implications for children involved in violence. In 2002, *Frontline* reported on several arms dealers, noting the following:

> Low-tech, handheld weapons and explosives do the vast majority of the killing today. There are more than 550 million small arms currently in circulation, many of them fueling bloody civil strife in countries from Sri Lanka to Sierra Leone.
>
> In most cases, the countries involved in these conflicts have been the subject of international embargoes imposed by the United Nations and other organizations. In some cases, major powers want to supply the side they favor in the conflict but do not want their "fingerprints" to be discovered on weapons of war.[43]

Since both Sri Lanka and Sierra Leone have a record of extensive use of child soldiers, it is important to recognize the role of arms dealers in perpetuating youth violence.

Profiting from Prisons

More than one in one hundred Americans are now behind bars.[44] For black men between the ages of 20 and 34, that number is one in nine. The International Center for Prison Studies at Kings College, London, provides statistics to indicate that this per capita rate of those behind bars is far higher than in any European country.[45] According to the Justice Reinvestment Project website, the amount that all states combined spend on prisons rose from about $12 billion in 1988 to about $52 billion in 2008.[46] California governor Arnold Schwarzenegger, in his 2010 State of the State Address, noted that prison spending had outpaced spending on higher education in his state.

> The priorities have become out of whack over the years. I mean, think about it. Thirty years ago 10 percent of the general fund went to higher education and three percent went to prisons. Today, almost 11 percent goes to prisons and only 7.5 percent goes to higher education.[47]

Thus, if one considers the economics of what to invest in, prisons would be a reasonably good choice. There is, as one might imagine, a trade group representing private correctional companies, the Association for Private Correctional and Treatment Organizations.[48] There still needs to be research and data collection tabulated regarding the relative quality of correctional services of for-profit organizations versus those of a state or federal government. Without young people needing these correctional and rehabilitative services, the privately owned companies would not post a profit. Recently, the Public Broadcasting System noted that one of the for-profit businesses that run both youth and adult prisons made $1.4 billion in profit in 2007.[49] The trade organization site advertises that private facilities save taxpayer money. This assertion creates interest in such facilities, especially in an economic downturn. Thorough analysis is still needed to ascertain whether these for-profit prisons are providing facilities that are adequate and the equivalent of those provided by the public sector. It would seem counterintuitive that a company could provide equal, much less superior, services while making a profit.

Beyond the service issue, however, is a more worrisome story, reported in early 2009 by both MSNBC and *The London Times*. *The London Times* reported that two Pennsylvania judges had pled guilty to accepting more than $2 million in "kickbacks" from the operators of juvenile detention centers, in exchange for their sentencing youth to those centers. One of the judges, Mark Ciavarella, sent an extremely high rate of youth to detention for seemingly minor actions, for example, a first offense of shoplifting a jar of nutmeg worth $4.[50] (Ciavarella has since been sentenced to 28 years in federal prison on felony corruption charges.[51])

Profiting from Child Prostitution

Pross was painfully stitched up so she could be resold as a virgin. In all, the brothel owner sold her virginity four times.[52]

Estimates of how many children [in the US] are involved in prostitution vary wildly—ranging from thousands to tens of thousands. More solid numbers do not exist, in part because the Department of Justice has yet to study the matter even though Congress authorized it to do so in 2005 as part of a nationwide study of the illegal commercial sex industry.[53]

A UN report from 1995 estimated that 2 million children under the age of 18 were engaged in prostitution worldwide. About 1 million were thought to be in Asia, and about 300,000 in the United States.[54]

Journalists Kristof and WuDunn[55] have brought attention to the economic aspect—the common "brothel business model"[56] as they put it—of forced prostitution. These are human traffickers who lie to and bribe parents and caretakers into giving up their children, usually girls, claiming that the girls will be educated when in fact they will be virtually imprisoned as prostitutes.

INTERNATIONALLY MARKETING FAUX-VIOLENT-URBAN AND HIP-HOP FASHION

The American urban, hip-hop, violent image, marketed throughout the world, is a highly sanitized version of the horrific reality of adolescents immersed in real urban violence. In the romanticized version, thugs get rich easily by virtue of their power, their identity, and their money, becoming, however improbably, irresistible to young women. In the very popular song "That's How You Like It," the products of at least two companies—Nike and Timberland—are named and associated with the "thug culture." Creative entrepreneurs have packaged urban fashion that sells clothing, shoes, boots, music, videos, bicycles, and cars—all with a hint of poverty, a hint of violence, a hint of prison—but without real poverty, real violence, or real prison. The adolescents immersed in real violence are at a real risk of being killed or imprisoned, but the sanitized, commercialized version of urban violence style, purchased at the mall, creates no risk greater than that of eye rolling by parents and teachers in suburban schools.

Executives at clothing empires are creating wealth for themselves by taking advantage of youth who have no real knowledge or experience of urban violence The romanticized, sanitized images they create are a façade that allows them to benefit from the status quo, regardless of how ugly that might be.

CONCLUSION

The lives of too many of the world's youth are immersed in violence. Although the scale of the problem may not be understood, any child who grows up in a violent milieu is cause for worry. Even those adults who are concerned and who try to intervene do not fully grasp the extent to which other adults benefit from youth violence and are seldom held accountable for it. Intervention with the individual child or family, through clinical methods, has not proven to be efficient, and most efforts probably represent a failure to recognize the scope as well as the realities of children immersed in violence all over the world. Those global citizens with some means must decide whether to continue to put their resources toward helping such children, one at a time—a feel-good solution—or whether as a society we have the courage to intervene against those who promote or benefit from violence.

The outlines of legislation, enforcement, and follow-up are becoming clearer through the efforts of the UN, the International Labor Organization, the Basel Convention, and other similar international bodies, along with the U.S. Congress. Some attempts at reducing child violence through prevention of profiteering have been weak or half-hearted. Some of the efforts that seemed promising have not been enacted, and others, though enacted, have not been enforced. It must be admitted that no action to change corruption and criminal activities can be achieved without citizen involvement. The first step for concerned citizens in developed countries is to explore the national and international laws, conventions, and proposals referred to in this chapter, as well as those available on the Internet, and decide which seem worthy of endorsement and of the time and effort to lobby lawmakers to pass new laws and enforce them—not to mention those that are already on the books.

Yet, it is not enough for concerned and involved groups to lobby their local, state, and federal agencies. The plight of so many suffering children, lost and alone, abandoned by adults, requires the strongest advocacy for change. It is a global problem worthy of attention from a worldwide audience. But networks start out on a local level and, once strong enough, join with others at a statewide level, with still others in a region and, ultimately, their message combines with those of like-minded citizen groups on a national or international stage. Youth violence will truly end only when the benefits gained from it by a few are unveiled for what they are— the manipulation of innocent, youth by persons and processes who view the youth merely as raw material to be used, just as any inanimate object might be used—for a profit that ultimately diminishes the humanity of all concerned.

Boston and Cambridge citizens had, in 2013, been deeply affected by the end result of the actions of scurrilous adults benefiting from the recruitment of youth who become immersed in violence. But we are only the most recent entrants into that large pool of concerned people, wondering how to intervene in time. That question is the focus of Chapter 5.

5

❖

Prevention of Future Terrorism

Since 9/11, the US war on terrorism has probably exceeded Al
Qaeda's best hopes for the power of jujitsu politics. A wall is rising
between Muslims and the West, Arabs and Muslims in the United
States are discriminated against.... US foreign policy has given people of many countries—not only Arabs and Muslims—reason to fear
and resent US power.

—Clark McCauley, 2006[1]

Never doubt that a small group of thoughtful, committed citizens
can change the world; indeed, it's the only thing that ever has.

—Margaret Mead

The individual has to wake up to the fact that violence cannot end
violence, that only understanding and compassion can neutralize
violence because, with the practice of loving speech and compassionate listening, you can begin to understand people and help people to remove the wrong perceptions in them because these wrong
perceptions are at the foundation of their anger, their fear, their violence, their hate. And listen deeply. You might be able to remove
the wrong perception you have within yourself concerning you and
concerning them. So the basic practice in order to remove terrorism
and war is the practice of removing wrong perceptions, and that cannot be done with the bombs and the guns. And it is very important

that our political leaders realize that and apply the techniques of communication.

—Thich Nhat Hanh[2]

This chapter contains a set of suggested actions that are likely to intervene in time to divert more good kids like Dzhokhar Tsarnaev, Hassan Abdi Dhuhulow, or Aymen Saadi from becoming deadly terrorists. As seen in Chapter 4, however, terrorism is but one special case of good kids being recruited, seduced, coerced, or threatened into lives immersed in violence. Intervening to prevent good kids from becoming terrorists will be part of a set of actions that help prevent good kids from becoming immersed in violence as victims or perpetrators of a variety of kinds of activities: prostitution, gang activity, drug sales, slavery, work with dangerous and toxic substances, and others. In the paragraphs that follow, the focus is on terrorism. But there is enough similarity in the process of recruitment to terrorism, recruitment to gangs, recruitment to rebel and mainstream militias, and recruitment to other dangerous forms of labor, that the general approach outlined here should be adaptable to any of those.

As one might imagine, attempts are being made in various parts of the world to dissuade youth from joining militias. There are undoubtedly many things being tried. On recommendation from the Russian security forces, the American Federal Bureau of Investigation (FBI) met with Tamerlan Tsarnaev to assess whether he posed a threat, but was not convinced that he did. The PST in Norway had some talks with Hassan Abdi Dhuhulow in an attempt to dissuade him from going to Somalia, and they regularly meet with youth they believe to be considering going to fight in other parts of the world (currently mainly in Syria), to dissuade them. In Colombia, there is some attempt to counter rebel forces' recruitment tactics with ad campaigns.[3] Some have suggested, and tried, providing youth with rewards for not being recruited. This is probably contraindicated by principles of psychology. The principle that is important here is that extrinsic rewards tend to destroy the potential for intrinsic motivation. That is, if youth are given money or objects as rewards for not signing up to join a terrorist organization, they will lose sight of the possible internal motivation, such as pride or development of prosocial identity or unwillingness to kill others, and in fact may later be more vulnerable to being recruited if the terrorist organization offers larger or more desirable rewards.

ROLE OF PARENTS AND OTHER FAMILY MEMBERS

Parents and other family members have a long-term responsibility to prepare their children for life in their communities. This includes providing for their children's needs, such as love, food, shelter, education, and guidance. Most would also agree that family members have a right to engage with and monitor nonfamily members who influence their children, including teachers, coaches, members of the clergy, and others. The sphere of influence, and the family members' control over that sphere, diminishes as the child gets older, though the pace and degree of that diminution varies a great deal by culture. Among the challenges for immigrant families in the United States is the different speed of assimilation. Parents are often shocked and dismayed to find that their children have become "American," and while earlier generations took pride in this transition, some contemporary immigrant parents find this an unwelcome development. In these situations it is tricky for all concerned to negotiate and renegotiate the level of influence that parents exert. This is especially true when children become more fluent in English than their parents, and thus are sometimes more aware and attuned to the immediate environment than their parents. This is an area for which there is no one-size-fits-all solution. But it is very important for communities—and for those of good will who would try to intervene to reduce the likelihood that kids will be vulnerable to recruitment—to be aware of the complex nature of the responsibility of families. If we consider the Tsarnaev family, we might wonder what would have happened if coaches, teachers, peers, or other community members had tried to engage Dzhokhar and Tamerlan in discussions about Islam. It seems likely, in the case of the Tsarnaev family, that the setting for such talks might have been school. Perhaps in most communities, efforts to discuss issues of importance to at-risk kids should take place as part of educational endeavors. In other communities it might be at places of worship or settings of civic engagement, such as community service settings.

In dozens of conversations with adolescents and college students in the 21st century, I have been told repeatedly that neither parents nor teachers know about many of the difficult and challenging decisions faced by adolescents, and that the adolescents keep this information from their parents so that their parents do not worry. This includes information about bullying, drug use, and sexual pressures, among other topics. Youth who are being recruited also often keep this information from their families, including parents, in order to protect the family members from worry, as well as to keep family members from prohibiting them from making their own decisions. Often, then, family members are not aware that their kids are being recruited, and the first they know about it may be when their children have departed to fight in what the kids see as a worthy cause.

In light of this, communities should neither blame parents for their children's decisions nor assume that parents alone can prevent their children from being recruited to terrorist activities. But it would be a mistake for adults in the community to create complicated programs or plans to engage youth in conversations without the involvement of parents. Indeed, many youth who are being recruited would benefit greatly from discussing the dilemmas they face with parents, assuming that parents are able to listen well and draw the youth out.

In all these efforts to find ways to help youth think carefully and critically about questions of recruitment, it would be helpful to consider how to get the youth to formulate and ask important questions. One approach that may be helpful to many communities is fostered by an organization called the "Right Question Institute." Part of the mission statement of this organization is to assist everyone "to learn to ask better questions and participate more effectively in decisions that affect them."[4] Imagine a 17-year-old who is being recruited mulling over questions like "How many kids are being recruited?" "Why me?" "What qualities do I have to offer that will benefit this organization?" "How will I, or my parents, be rewarded for my service?" "Will my service cause others to be harmed?" "What will my tasks be?" "Where will I work?" "What options do I have if I change my mind?" "How long will I be expected to provide services?" "What other ways might I have to help this cause?" "Can I provide more help if I continue my education and become an attorney, or a translator, rather than dying in an attack?" "How will this decision affect my parents?"

IDENTIFYING KIDS AT RISK OF RECRUITMENT

The short version of this section is that it is impossible to identify kids at risk and only kids at risk of recruitment. If we take the alleged Boston Marathon bombers, for example, Dzhokhar would simply not have been identified. Indeed, he was noted to have a "heart of gold" by an elementary school teacher.[5] His high school wrestling coach treated him like a son. Teachers and peers at Cambridge Rindge and Latin School saw him as compassionate, chill, a great friend. His wrestling team elected him captain two years in a row. Yet unbeknownst to all of them, he was at risk. Undoubtedly we could find other kids who were thought to be at risk, but who found reasons and ways to desist from problematic activities on their own. Any method we might have now of identifying kids at risk is likely to include many errors in both directions: we would miss some kids who are actually at risk, and we would incorrectly identify some kids who are not at risk. The best approach, then, is to see to it that all kids have opportunities to receive the kind of attention, connection, conversation, engagement, and inoculation that will help them resist the seductive promises of recruiters.

It seems that some stages in the recruitment process may involve young people self-selecting, possibly having been encouraged by friends or peers, to watch recruitment videos, read jihadist websites, and so on.[6] Still, even if they initiate contact or participate in recruitment voluntarily by watching recruitment videos, or if they just show up unsolicited at the border of Syria to participate in war, kids are being screened by the recruiters they contact, and those recruiters are tailoring their efforts to the kids with special talents and special vulnerabilities. Youth are likely to be assigned to one of a variety of roles within the movement based on these vulnerabilities and abilities. As noted in Chapter 2, for example, youth who seem to have mental illness are unlikely to be welcome to fight in a group that depends on them for the action to go smoothly. If they are not seen as reliable, they will likely be assigned to roles where they are disposable, whereas others who are able to be relied upon may be assigned to work that requires cooperation and/or planning and preparation. Many of the recruits, including the best and brightest, who have so much to contribute to society, are also recognized as having much to contribute to the effort. Many are having their futures cut short—to the detriment of themselves, their families, their communities, and the world—by their actions, which will result in death or lives in hiding, or in prison. Recruiters may be delighted to have such good kids volunteer for actions in their home countries, because they can prepare to engage in deadly actions without arousing suspicion, just as Dzhokhar Tsarnaev seems to have done.[7]

Recruiters who get kids to become immersed in violence expend a lot of effort to do so. An equal amount of work is required to take steps toward inoculating youth against readily agreeing to be recruited. These counter recruitment efforts should include opportunities for meaningful lives, including opportunities to work for causes of their choice. Some kids, like Dzhokhar Tsarnaev, have many facets of identity. For them, opportunities to explore these facets, integrate them, and make a meaningful life that incorporates their various alliances may be needed.

The effort to counter-recruit will require a no-drama assessment of where the West stands, and how that looks to kids with complex identities and loyalties.

SURVEILLANCE, SECURITY, AND DISCRIMINATION: NEW NORMS?

For several years after September 11, 2001, it was common for thoughtful Americans of good will to express horror, worry, and distress over the U.S. counterterrorism policies and the effects on immigrants, Arabs, Muslims, and people who are incorrectly identified as immigrants, Arabs or Muslims.

It seems that over the decade since the start of the controversial Iraq War, now more or less over, and the Afghanistan War, now winding down, Americans have become weary of war, and also weary of protesting, and have accepted a kind of new norm in which violent American intervention in the Middle East is an uncomfortable fact of life, and in which people who look like Arab or Muslims are targeted routinely for "random" checks at airports and detained for hours on end at the U.S.-Canada border without explanation. This inching toward complacency with the status quo is creating danger for the United States and other Western countries, as youth who see injustices and discrimination and do not see adults protesting it are likely to assume that the policy reflects the sentiments of all—or at least many or most—Americans. And recruiters are able to make a case for Americans in general being insensitive, uncaring, and even hateful toward others. Imagine a Muslim teenager, witnessing her parents treated unfairly, in subtle ways, and also learning about drone strikes in mostly Muslim countries, with citizens of those countries afraid and governments protesting, but the United States continuing to use drones. Imagine hearing the U.S. government claiming that the drone strikes are accurate and even "surgical," and seeing hardly any public protests by Americans. Imagine that you are a Third Culture Kid, as discussed in Chapter 3, trying to deal with conflict between your home country and the United States. Imagine now you are deciding how to live a meaningful life. Imagine your uncle telling you to join the U.S. military. You might really need someone to talk to about all of this. And where would you turn?

GOOD KIDS HAVE A LOT TO TALK ABOUT—WHO'S LISTENING?

When we examine the lives of kids who later become recruited into violence, we often find kids like Dzhokhar Tsarnaev, who seem to be doing well. Upon closer analysis, we often find, as with Dzhokhar, that no one really knows them intimately. No one suspects they are troubled. Or perhaps some people notice that they seem somewhat distressed or upset, but no one asks the hard questions, or sticks around to hear the troubling answers. In the early news reports about the Boston Marathon bombings, there were several people who knew the Tsarnaevs who alluded to brief conversations that could have led to greater understanding of their dilemmas and might have led to invitations to talk further. In each case, the person reporting was either satisfied with an answer that amounted to a brushoff or taken aback by an unexpected response and did not pursue the conversation. If Cambridge has to ask itself some hard questions, the first,

I think, is why no one talked and listened to Dzhokhar long enough or personally enough to understand what he was going through. The second is why no one realized that he would be at risk of being recruited, and helped him to see, in the clear light of day, what that would mean for his life.

It seems possible, based on reports that Dzhokhar was typically able to get away with breaking laws and failing courses by some combination of lying and acting remorseful,[8] that he may have thought he could actually get away with the Boston Marathon bombings without being caught. This would have to assume that he had somehow misjudged the level of expertise of U.S. law enforcement agencies, and the high priority placed on pursuing terrorists. It would have to assume that he somehow forgot about surveillance cameras, or believed that his reputation as a good kid would cause others to vindicate him. If all that were true, improbable as it seems, it would explain why he did not attempt any sort of disguise or any sort of cover, but wore his hat backward, with no sunglasses or other cover, when depositing his backpack at the finish line. And since no one was talking with him, or listening to him, no one was able to discuss with him the likely consequences of engaging in the bombings, or to help him question the promise of martyrdom and the promises of its rewards in an afterlife. No one was able to suggest to him that he had other ways of being helpful to the causes he held dear or to suggest what some of those ways might be or to suggest that he at least defer his decision until he explored some other options.

This is an invitation to any and all adults of good will living in countries affected by terrorism, and that includes virtually every adult in the world. Do something yourself, rather than waiting for your government, or the United Nations, or a future world leader, or a security force such as the NSA, Secret Service, MI5, or PST to find a way to end or reduce the incidence of good kids becoming deadly terrorists. Bring together like-minded neighbors, friends, and other community members, and gain support from the town council, or the local high school, or the local interfaith council and make a plan to reach out to youth at risk in your community. It is the intention of this book in general, and this chapter in particular, to inspire you to act—and soon—and to provide some suggestions about where to start. While spy agencies spy, military organizations fight, humanitarian organizations provide aid, and government officials mull over policy decisions, you can do something today, in your town, in your neighborhood, on your block, that will contribute to ending this worrisome recruitment of good kids into lives of violence by ambitious and uncaring adults who will use them as weapons to cause senseless suffering and pain.

In order to reach kids before a recruiter reaches them, you will have to be proactive. And since terrorist incidents are low frequency, and the goal is to keep them that way, you will have to be willing and able to do this without kudos. No one is going to thank you for preventing terrorism.

Here are the four principles to follow when you decide to act:

1. Listen and talk to the kids in your life in a serious, drama-free way. Do not shy away from kids with problems or from hard subjects. Find out about their lives, their interests, their passions, their pasts. Engage their parents. In work my colleagues and students and I have done with kids who are doing well, with those who are in trouble with the law, with kids who are born in the United States, with those who are immigrants, with kids who have never faced difficulty, with those who have been traumatized, and with poor kids and affluent ones, the feedback we receive repeatedly is that the most valuable aspect of working with mentors, student interns, and professionals was that they had someone to talk to, apart from their families. These were not kids who hated their families or whose parents were mean or abusive. They were just kids. Often the best way to start these conversations is around a shared project or activity. This is why coaches, teachers, mentors, and others often learn so much about the kids they work with. While listening and asking kids about their lives, you do not have to provide guidance, or instruction, or discipline. Just listen with what the Public Conversations Project calls "Genuine Curiosity."[9] Be honest and open, but do not try to change the kids' minds, or even to read the kids' minds. Let them know you are available to hear more and to help if you can. A few cautionary notes here. If you do not already do so, do not take kids into your home, or provide any money or things of value as incentive. The value is in your being interested and listening. If you want to pay for tea or lunch, that is ok. But do not loan money or give large gifts, as these will distract from the core function here, which is connection.

2. Get together with other concerned adults, including adults of every race, religion, and ethnicity represented in your community, to figure out how to reach the kids who are not talking to anyone. This effort should be inclusive, and may require delicate conversations with families who are not connected to the community as of yet. It should include kids who are doing well and those who are not doing so well. I am not recommending psychotherapy for all these kids, but only additional connections with adults who care about their well-being. Discuss together the goals

of your project—to get kids connected to the community. One way to do this is to provide ways for kids to make an impact on their world positively, to receive recognition for that, and to help others, younger than themselves, to do so as well. Let them know that they can help the cause of social justice. This is especially important for kids who are disillusioned, who do not like what their community or country is doing, who know there is unfairness, and who do not see adults addressing it. To be perfectly clear here, kids of good will who see injustice want to see it fixed, and all the better if they can be involved in fixing it. This is the very motive that causes many young people to become engaged in violence and terrorism to begin with: they see no other way to make a meaningful statement and make an impact. Provide real ways they can create change in their neighborhood, school, and community. Keep in mind that even kids who experience no discrimination directed at them are often hurt and distressed by seeing others be victimized, whether next door or thousands of miles away. Adults are often tempted to dismiss these concerns as adolescent idealism—something that kids will grow out of once they learn how the real world works. Sadly, some of those kids will not live long enough to find out how the world works, because in their misguided efforts to change it, they will be recruited by unscrupulous, uncaring adults who, promising them an opportunity for a meaningful life and a meaningful death, will use them to bolster the adults' own fortunes.

3. In your interfaith, interethnic group, discuss the real possibility that some of the kids in your community will have to face the possibility of being recruited, by other kids or adults either nearby or halfway across the world, to engage in violence of one kind or another. The lesson of this book is that any kids, including good kids with promising futures, may be recruited. Psychologists have learned that inoculation, training, and practice work. That is, having an open conversation with kids about what they may see, hear, and experience is likely to be helpful to many kids. Discussions and role-plays about the possibility of recruitment will also help. Watching segments of recruitment videos should also be considered. Kids should not have to face these prospects unprepared. In my mind, these recruiters engage in a form of child abuse, and kids should be as well prepared to deal with them as they are prepared today to avoid being kidnaped, raped, or otherwise abused by family members or strangers.

It is absolutely critical that all faiths, races, and ethnicities collaborate on this part of the project, since no one person understands the realities of all the smaller groups in the community. How might a white middle-class person speak to a young black man, trying to prepare him for the temptations of gang membership? How likely is it that a young Muslim will be convinced by a Christian adult that they should resist becoming part of a rebel group in the Syrian war? Your group may want to have consultants from communities not well represented in your group, or from local youth leaders or town officials, or from clergy, law enforcement, or scholars.

Your interfaith, interethnic group may want to work with groups of kids, rather than individual kids, in doing this inoculation, training, and practice. Each community will have to make its decisions as appropriate for that community.

4. You, and all the adults in your group, must now become as globally aware as the kids you talk to. If they are concerned about the war in Syria, you will have to learn about it. If they see injustice and want to address it, you will also have to learn about it. It is not necessary for you to be an activist. But you can help if you know of some legitimate, safe, activist groups to which the kids you talk to may want to become connected. Some examples may be local chapters of well-regarded humanitarian groups, or well-regarded antiwar groups, or nonprofit community groups that the kids can engage with. Some of the kids you talk to may want to work with missionaries, or aid groups. Some may become convinced that they will be better able to serve a just cause by completing their education before becoming active.

If you are looking for some good sourcebooks for talking to kids with genuine curiosity, even with kids whose values and actions you may not understand or approve, I suggest checking out some of the books in the annotated reference list at the end of this book. A starting point might be the following nonfiction works: *Teens Who Hurt* by Hardy and Lazsloffy,[10] *Fist Stick Knife Gun* by Geoffrey Canada,[11] *Rethinking Juvenile Justice* by Scott and Steinberg,[12] and *Difficult Conversations* by Stone, Patton, and Heen.[13] In addition, good windows into the hearts and minds of kids who are immersed in violence include fiction such as *Man's Fate* by Andre Malraux,[14] *Terrorist* by John Updike,[15] and *Bel Canto* by Ann Patchett.[16]

REMOVING OBSTACLES

The actions I am suggesting might well bring citizens to the attention of local, state, and/or national law enforcement. In the current security climate in the United States, any and all groups—including humanitarian agencies—may find themselves under surveillance, as security concerns seem to overwhelm privacy concerns. Three sets of actions are recommended to address that possibility. The first is to be proactive in engaging local officials to assist in your adult group, perhaps even asking them to endorse the project, once the group has been formed and discussions are underway. The second is to lobby your state and local officials, as well as educators and scholars, to endorse and assist with the general goals of working with youth in a prevention model. The third is getting legal advice about the nature of your good will endeavors in order not to inadvertently create difficulties.

In acknowledging the possibility that the actions I suggest may bring government scrutiny, I want to state clearly that I think such scrutiny is a reflection of the freedom versus security pendulum swinging so far toward security that it undermines the very security it seeks to establish. A few years after September 11, 2001, a group of psychologists published a book called *Collateral Damage*,[17] in which they detailed how the U.S. government's response to the terror attacks was itself causing damage that, in some cases, topped the damage done by the attacks themselves. That problem seems to be continuing today, as we have recently seen the damage to business and international relations done by what is arguably excessive and evidently unnecessary surveillance by the NSA, by reports first of interrogations and torture at Guantanamo, and now of deaths of civilians by drone strikes. All these and more have become very effective recruiting tools for anti-American groups, including those who advocate violence.

As the United States rebalances its emphasis on security via surveillance following a recent review panel appointed by President Obama,[18] perhaps a friendlier atmosphere may ultimately prevail, one in which concerned citizens, meeting together in an interfaith, interethnic community group with the goal of helping youth face the challenge of recruitment to terrorism, would not be in danger of being scrutinized, or of being suspected of being a threat to U.S. security.

It is possible, then, that for now, people meeting out of good will to assist kids at risk may find themselves in situations similar to those of the youth they plan to help—objects of surveillance and suspicion. Despite these risks, it is likely to be a help to kids and families, demonstrating to them that others care, that they have a place in the community, and that youth have a part to play in assuring social justice.

AND IN THE LONG RUN, STOPPING RECRUITERS

Ultimately, communities should identify recruiters who bring kids into lives of violence. Undoubtedly, there are some recruiters who actually believe that the youth are going to benefit from becoming immersed in violence as victims or perpetrators or both. Perhaps they believe the youth will be better protected or cared for than if they were on the streets alone. Or perhaps they believe in the cause they are recruiting for, and truly appreciate the sacrifices being made by the youth. Perhaps they falsely believe that it is fair to capitalize on youthful idealism. However, in most cases around the world (and I include here all recruiters, not only those who recruit with promises of spiritual or religious redemption, but also those who recruit child soldiers, drug runners, servants, sexual companions, and so on) the beneficiaries are the recruiters. Having identified those who engage in such recruitment efforts, communities must put them out of business. Perhaps the best-known spokesperson for this point of view is *New York Times* columnist Nicholas Kristof, author, with Sheryl WuDunn, of the popular book about women around the world, called *Half the Sky*.[19] Even Kristof found that in some situations, the recruiters of youth and the owners of slaves are complex people with some tenderness. Like the Madam in Steinbeck's *Cannery Row*,[20] some take care of the needs of the younger prostitutes, and see to it that the brothel is run according to some sort of personal standards of dignity.

In light of all this, putting recruiters out of business is going to help youth at risk of future recruitment, while it may be disruptive to some extent for youth already recruited. In each instance, those who put the recruiters out of business will also be responsible for seeing to the needs of the youth already recruited. In the case of drug runners, for example, putting the suppliers out of business will leave some youth vulnerable to angry customers who, deprived of their drug of choice, may be irrational and unpredictable. When recruiters of prostitutes are put out of business, some of the girls already recruited will be left with no source of support or income and may perhaps have no way home. In addition they may be worried about whether they will be welcome back home if they do find a way to get there. Some of the principles of disarming, demobilizing, and reintegrating child soldiers (DDR) may apply to youth in these situations as well. Principles of DDR include recognizing that the needs of former female child soldiers differ from those of former male child soldiers.

AND FOR THE GOVERNMENT: TALKING TO TERRORISTS

A sure way for a politician in the United States to attract criticism is to suggest talking to terrorist organizations as a means to attain long-term peace. As Zen Buddhist Monk and peace activist Thich Naht Hanh, among many other wise people, suggests, in the long run this is a necessary step. The world has some good examples of how this works, such as in Northern Ireland and in South Africa. In both cases, government officials and leaders of terrorist groups negotiated peace. In both cases it was very hard, and not universally popular while it was going on. In both cases, the leaders negotiating were at grave risk. In the long run, in both cases, the United States celebrated the end of conflict.

Still, politicians who suggest anything like this for the United States are sure to be verbally attacked by their opponents, and possibly also by members of their own party. Refusal to talk omits perhaps the only viable option for peace. While Nelson Mandela was praised by virtually every commentator in the United States following his death, it would be wise for all of us to remember that there was a time—less than three decades ago—when Nelson Mandela and the militant branch of the African National Congress were condemned as terrorists.[21] Much has changed since then. Now it would be hard to find anyone in the United States who would debate the importance of a democratic South Africa where people of all races vote. How did South Africa become a relatively peaceful democracy? It was because the government and the terrorist organization talked to each other and negotiated peace.

This year (2014), we see a possible end to terrorism in Colombia, as the president of that nation is beginning talks with terrorist organizations there. Juan Manuel Santos explains his reasoning in a short article in the *Wall Street Journal*, titled "Why I'm Talking to Terrorists in Colombia."[22]

DOES THIS JUSTIFY RECRUITMENT?

Here we enter some complicated territory. The UN takes the stand that anyone under 18 is a child, and if recruited to a militia, becomes a child soldier. But what of 18 year olds who are recruited to perform actions that are not standard military actions, but that will deliberately do three things: (1) kill innocent civilians; (2) end the youths' potential for productive lives, since, if they are caught, they will be imprisoned; and (3) very likely end their lives by death as a consequence of the action? And what if they recruit these youth with promises of special status in the afterlife or even in this life?

While I would, somewhat reluctantly, agree that an 18-year-old has the agency to decide whether to join a military or even a militia, I also believe that all youth, including young adults, are entitled to the recruitment being open, public, and able to be publicly discussed. And I strongly believe that all youth have the right to be warned and prepared for the possibility of recruitment, and to have a chance to discuss with many others, not only with the recruiter, the pros and cons of agreeing to be recruited.

There is no way we can stop all youth from agreeing to be recruited. But we can bring the recruitment process into daylight and also help adolescents and young adults weigh out the possible consequences to themselves, their families, and their communities, should they agree to join a cause, a militia, or a terrorist organization. This open discussion will likely reduce the thrill, excitement, and grand promises of recruitment, at the same time that it will enable the youth to fully consider the potential negative long-term consequences of recruitment, something that neuroscience has shown is not easy or natural for youth, who tend to overestimate short-term gains and underestimate long-term costs when making decisions, including life-altering decisions.

IMAGINING A BETTER FUTURE

Is it possible that some day in the United States, it will be hard to find anyone who would debate the importance of hard-won respect for all who are adherents to Islam? This may be as hard for us to believe today as it was hard to believe that we would one day consider it ridiculous to think that Catholics, Jews, and people of color should be respected as equals to white Anglo-Saxon protestant men, that women should attend college and be employed in the workforce, that gays should have a right to marry, or that interracial marriages should be celebrated. Hard as it is to grasp, we may even one day see a president tell the Israeli prime minister to "tear down that wall," and an Israeli prime minister who might do so, because there might no longer be a threat of terrorism.

As we will see in Chapter 6, the trajectory of the human race over millennia supports these possible future developments. Specifically, in the last half-century or so, great gains have been made by the international community in recognition of human rights. `

6

Reviewing the Seville Statement: Humans Are Not Naturally Violent

[I]t is essential, if man is not to be compelled to have recourse, as a last resort, to rebellion against tyranny and oppression, that human rights should be protected by the rule of law.
—Preamble to the Universal Declaration of Human Rights, 1948[1]

IT IS SCIENTIFICALLY INCORRECT to say that war or any other violent behavior is genetically programmed into our human nature.
—Second Proposition, Seville Statement, 1986

[F]or all the cruelty and hardship of our world, we are not mere prisoners of fate. Our actions matter, and can bend history in the direction of justice.
—President Barack Obama, on receiving the Nobel Peace Prize, 2009[2]

Left to their own devices, humans will not fall into a state of peaceful cooperation, but nor do they have a thirst for blood that must regularly be slaked.
—Steven Pinker, 2011[3]

Aggression is not at the core of human nature, and human evolution did not produce a particularly violent species called *Homo sapiens*. The popular media and a portion of the academic literature may present this picture, but it is not an accurate representation of our evolutionary history or how we act in our everyday lives.

—Agustín Fuentes, 2012[4]

One way to contribute toward the transformation of a culture of war into a culture of peace is to shift attitudes, values, and behavior to promote peace and social justice, and the nonviolent resolution of conflict.

—J. Martin Ramirez, 2014[5]

HOW NATURAL IS VIOLENCE?

News of terrorism, war, slavery, rape, and homicide fill headlines and news reports across the entire United States on a daily basis. This news demands our attention, and causes us distress, fear, and sometimes despair. It seems, based on our daily experience of news, that humans must surely be inescapably doomed to violence. Alternative news sources—those that publish inspiring stories and good news, as well as those that criticize unfair and discriminatory practices—have been around for some time, and have gained in popularity recently, with one news source, called Upworthy, currently achieving considerable publicity due to its success in a short time with a tight budget.[6] Yet even the most popular good news sources get a very tiny amount of attention in comparison with mainstream news sources, the latter featuring just a few feel-good stories among the nearly steady stream of violence, disaster, and despair. Despite the attention that bad news gets in newscasts, however (a common cliché about newsrooms is "if it bleeds, it leads"), violence does not fill most of our daily lives, most of the time, as noted by Agustín Fuentes in the quote mentioned earlier. Indeed, violence is noteworthy, and thus newsworthy, because it is out of the ordinary.

The answer to the question of how "natural" it is to be violent should lead to decisions that affect the very nature of our society. If it were human destiny, and human instinct, based on our genetic makeup, to be violent, then, some might conclude, we may as well tolerate a society where the strongest, most aggressive, and most selfish survive and thrive, where everyone is spying on one another, and where a kind of institutionalized "One Percent Doctrine"[7] prevails, justifying extreme actions in the name of security, no matter whether they support or violate individual privacy or human rights. If, on the other hand, we are not destined to be violent, then those who care about the fate of their loved ones, and especially the fate of future generations, are tasked with creating some paths to reduction of violence in our communities, and taking action to encourage peace.

Data from psychology, sociology, criminal justice, anthropology, history—indeed the whole range of social sciences—provides hope, rather than despair. The findings from contemporary social science converge on evidence that humans have the potential for violence, and also the potential for nonviolence. Furthermore, they agree on the conditions that foster less of some kinds of violence (e.g., revenge killing). Violence is not genetically programmed to dominate our nature, and the data about violence indicates that people need not release pent-up anger or frustration through violence. In other words, violence is not an inevitable part of being human. Still more surprising to many, a good deal of carefully reviewed, empirical evidence indicates that the level of violence, measured in homicide, deaths by war, and other forms of violence, while it varies a good deal across time and cultures, has gone down considerably over the millennia of human existence.[8] As if to underscore this point, in cities across the United States, crime and homicide numbers have gone down in 2013.[9] In addition, the number of police officers killed by gunfire in the United States in 2013 is the lowest in over one hundred years, since 1887.[10] Indeed, gun violence and homicides have been on a downward trend in the United States since 1993. However, polling by the Pew Research Center shows that Americans are not aware of that trend. In fact, 56 percent of Americans think that the incidence of gun crimes has gone up in the last 20 years.[11]

Given the reduction of violence over time, and given that we are not doomed to violence, it seems it is incumbent on people of good will to try to understand what factors are relevant to reducing violence in the 21st century, to look for ways to continue (and perhaps enhance) the downward trend, and to cultivate the peaceful side of our natures. While violence continues on its downward trajectory then, we may consider whether we can manage with less burdensome security measures.

EFFORTS TO REDUCE VIOLENCE IN THE 20TH AND 21ST CENTURIES

While the trajectory of humankind is toward a reduction in violence and homicides over millennia, our recent history has presented some new challenges, including genocide, large-scale wars (World War I and World War II), a series of terrorist attacks, and the development and proliferation of nuclear weapons.[12] These events have already defined, and will continue to define, efforts to contain, reduce, and eliminate violence.

Indeed, given that we, collectively, have the capacity to end human civilization with nuclear weapons, efforts to reduce war and violence should continue to be very high on our priority list. I am not, here, suggesting that we immediately close down our police forces and mothball our entire military apparatus. Rather, I am suggesting that, in every community, peace should be sought with the conviction that it can be achieved. Perhaps a community that is totally free of violence will always be aspirational; still it is clear that, with thought and planning, we can make some progress. As President Obama said in his Nobel Peace Prize acceptance speech, "we are not mere prisoners of fate."[13]

First we might examine some of the worldwide efforts that have already taken place, and that have helped reduce violence, either directly or indirectly through improvement of human rights.

20TH-CENTURY CONCERNS

People in many parts of the world were horrified by the awfulness of war in the early 20th century—The Great War. (We now refer to that war as World War I, but at the time, it was unthinkable that there would be another war of such proportions. It was thought to be the war to end all wars, and thus called the Great War.) World War II destroyed much of Europe, and resulted in extremely high levels of deaths of young men in the military as well as of civilians. People of the Western world, horrified by loss and destruction, and yet relieved by the turn of events that led to victory over genocidal leaders, engaged, with great urgency, in debates about whether violence was an inevitable part of human nature. It seems that they were not aware of the general diminution of violence over time, but even if they had been aware of it, they would have wondered whether the World Wars were a sign that humans were regressing.

Two historically important developments during the post–World War II era are worthy of considering as both reflections and definitions of human commitment toward the reduction of violence. One is the Nuremberg Trials, a milestone that reflected an aspiration for humanity to move from the practice of brutal war and informal or even impulsive revenge (some called for immediate deaths to all Nazi leaders) to more formal and nuanced consideration of evidence and application of justice by a larger group, in this case, representatives of the four countries that made up the Allied Forces. Thus, as noted in chapter one, in the opening statement of the trials, Robert Jackson noted, and the world witnessed, "one of the most significant tributes that Power has ever paid to Reason."[14]

The other crucial post–World War II development is the adoption of the Universal Declaration of Human Rights in 1948. This declaration arguably laid the groundwork for several decades of continuing evolution of human rights for all, including persons and groups that had previously been seen as less than human and/or unworthy of human rights. A recent article by William Schulz, president of the Unitarian Universalist Service Committee, reminds readers that in 1948, when the Universal Declaration of Human Rights was signed, racial segregation in the United States and apartheid in South Africa were in place. We might add that gays' and lesbians' rights were limited, religious intolerance was condoned, and women were seen as having psychiatric problems if they wanted to work outside the home.[15] Psychologist Steven Pinker provides evidence of the increased attention to human rights, by graphing the use of various terms referring to "rights," such as "gay rights" and "women's rights" in literature during the 20th century.[16] He goes on to remind us that the increase in attention to the idea of rights parallels a decrease in violence toward those who are the beneficiaries of attention to rights. For example, along with civil rights for African Americans came a steep decline in the number of lynchings.[17]

The Nuremberg Trials and the Universal Declaration of Human Rights, taken together, reflect the recognition by those who had lived through World War II, that by guaranteeing human rights, we might prevent violence. The trials protected the rights of the accused, thus setting a very public example of respect for the rights of even the most despised persons, and protection of those persons, and the community at large, from uncontrolled revenge. The Declaration clearly reflected, as will be seen in the Preamble in the next section, the belief that, if you want peace, you should work for justice.

THE CONNECTION BETWEEN HUMAN RIGHTS AND PEACE, AS NOTED IN THE PREAMBLE TO THE UNIVERSAL DECLARATION OF HUMAN RIGHTS

Periodic review of the Universal Declaration of Human Rights is highly useful. The Declaration is readily available online. The following excerpt from the Preamble, however, serves as a reminder that, back in 1948, it was widely recognized, and widely endorsed, that human rights were essential to peace:

> Whereas recognition of the inherent dignity and of the equal and inalienable rights of all members of the human family is the foundation of freedom, justice and peace in the world,

Whereas disregard and contempt for human rights have resulted in barbarous acts which have outraged the conscience of mankind, and the advent of a world in which human beings shall enjoy freedom of speech and belief and freedom from fear and want has been proclaimed as the highest aspiration of the common people,

Whereas it is essential, if man is not to be compelled to have recourse, as a last resort, to rebellion against tyranny and oppression, that human rights should be protected by the rule of law. . . .[18]

It is a tribute to the wisdom of the drafters of this document that they recognized, even in 1948, that attention to human rights is crucial to prevention or reduction of violence and war. Research over the decades since 1948 has substantiated this observation. Sadly, however, reactions to the terrorist events of 2001 led, in many cases, to reduction, rather than enhancement, of human rights. Indeed, Arabs and Muslims were too often treated as suspect simply because of their identity. We would do well to remember the words of the Universal Declaration of Human Rights.

SCIENTISTS AS ACTIVISTS: THE ESTABLISHMENT OF PUGWASH

Also following the end of World War II, society set about dealing with the reality of nuclear weapons. Soon, with acquisition and stockpiling, the human race would have the potential to destroy itself by actions taken within a few minutes. Many wondered aloud whether there was any hope for the survival of society. Albert Einstein himself questioned whether humanity could survive without an international body with power to enforce its rules, and a great many physicists were chagrined that their beloved science had now spawned the most deadly weapons imaginable.

Pugwash is an organization whose purpose is to reduce the likelihood of war and violent conflict, with a special focus on avoiding nuclear war. Established in the 1950s, and including renowned scientists as well as policymakers, its mission is not to participate in formal negotiations among officials, but to foster discussions among scientists and officials. Pugwash describes it as follows:

The purpose of the Pugwash Conferences is to bring together, from around the world, influential scholars and public figures concerned with reducing the danger of armed conflict and seeking cooperative solutions for global problems. Meeting in private as individuals, rather than as representatives of governments or institutions, Pugwash participants exchange views and explore alternative approaches to arms control and tension reduction with a combination of candor, continuity, and flexibility seldom attained in official East-West and North-South discussions and negotiations. Yet, because of the stature of many of the Pugwash participants in their own countries (as, for example, science and arms-control advisers to governments, key figures in academies of science and universities, and former and future holders of high government office), insights from Pugwash discussions tend to penetrate quickly to the appropriate levels of official policy-making.[19]

That Pugwash has been deemed successful is reflected in the granting of the Nobel Peace Prize to Pugwash, and its first secretary general, Joseph Rotblat[20], in 1995, "for their efforts to diminish the part played by nuclear arms in international politics and, in the longer run, to eliminate such arms."[21, 22] Rotblat was the only scientist to leave the Manhattan Project on the grounds of conscience. He was a signatory of the Russell-Einstein Manifesto,[23] and a critic of the nuclear arms race. Given all these efforts from the period following World War II, we should be aware that in seeking to reduce violence and war, we are in the best of company.

ATTEMPTS TO UNDERSTAND HUMAN NATURE IN THE MIDST OF THE NUCLEAR ERA

The 1980s was an era when the possibility of nuclear war was on the minds of many in the Western world. It appears, in retrospect, that this was with good reason. U.S. president Reagan held strongly to anti-Communist perspectives, and referred to the Soviets as the Evil Empire. There was a time during 1983 when the U.S. and the Soviet Union actually came quite close to using nuclear weapons. Nuclear war was seen to be a real threat in real time, rather than in some imagined future.

In response, researchers explored how children and families viewed the possibility of nuclear war, and advised parents on how to help children avoid being harmed by awareness of the possibility of nuclear war. Films such as *The Day After* brought home the reality of the results of possible nuclear war.[24] Activists brought awareness and pressure to bear on government officials, hoping to support efforts at nuclear disarmament. And scientists, such as the signatories of the Seville Statement, did exhaustive reviews of available knowledge about human nature, with an eye toward determining whether violence, and perhaps even the destruction of civilization by violence, was such an entrenched part of being human that deadly war was inevitable.

In the 1980s, a group of more than 20 highly regarded scientists from all over the world studied whether violence was programmed into our genes, and concluded that humans are not doomed to violent behavior and war by our biological makeup, nor by our psychological makeup. After several years of study, this group came together at the sixth conference of the Coloquio Internacional sobre Cerebro y Agresión, (the International Colloquium on Conflict and Aggression, or CICA) in 1986, which was also the United Nations International Year of Peace, and prepared for release a document known as the *Seville Statement*. The United Nations Educational, Scientific, and Cultural Organization, UNESCO, adopted the Seville Statement in 1989. The statement is reproduced in its entirety below, followed by a review of contemporary commentary and analysis on the questions it answers.

As is evident from the opening quotes of this chapter, contemporary scientists' conclusions are in agreement with the Seville Statement: despite wars, violent media, and everyday violence in communities, humans are not genetically programmed for violence, and evolution does not favor the most aggressive members of the human community for survival. In short, humans have potential for aggression and potential for peace. Nonscientific wisdom also endorses this view. Take, for example, the often-told Cherokee story of the grandfather instructing his grandson about the human potential for peace or violence. The grandfather likens the potential inside himself to wolves—one good and one evil. He says that there is a fight going on between them. When the grandson asks which one wins, the grandfather replies, "The one I feed." This response is consistent with contemporary science: humans can foster violence or peace in themselves and in their communities.

THE SEVILLE STATEMENT

Introduction

Believing that it is our responsibility to address from our particular disciplines the most dangerous and destructive activities of our species, violence and war; recognising that science is a human cultural product which cannot be definitive or all encompassing; and gratefully acknowledging the support of the authorities of Seville and representatives of the Spanish UNESCO, we, the undersigned scholars from around the world and from relevant sciences, have met and arrived at the following Statement on Violence. In it, we challenge a number of alleged biological findings that have been used, even by some in our disciplines, to justify violence and war. Because the alleged findings have contributed to an atmosphere of pessimism in our time, we submit that the open, considered rejection of these misstatements can contribute significantly to the International Year of Peace. Misuse of scientific theories and data to justify violence and war is not new but has been made since the advent of modern science. For example, the theory of evolution has been used to justify not only war, but also genocide, colonialism, and suppression of the weak. We state our position in the form of five propositions. We are aware that there are many other issues about violence and war that could be fruitfully addressed from the standpoint of our disciplines, but we restrict ourselves here to what we consider a most important first step.

First Proposition

IT IS SCIENTIFICALLY INCORRECT to say that we have inherited a tendency to make war from our animal ancestors. Although fighting occurs widely throughout animal species, only a few cases of destructive intraspecies fighting between organised groups have ever been reported among naturally living species, and none of these involve the use of tools designed to be weapons. Normal predatory feeding upon other species cannot be equated with intraspecies violence. Warfare is a peculiarly human phenomenon and does not occur in other animals. The fact that warfare has changed so radically over time indicates that it is a product of culture. Its biological connection is primarily through language which makes possible the co-ordination of groups, the transmission of technology, and the use of tools. War is biologically possible, but it is not inevitable, as evidenced by its variation in occurrence and nature over time and space. There are cultures which have not engaged in war for centuries, and there are cultures which have engaged in war frequently at some times and not at others.

Second Proposition

IT IS SCIENTIFICALLY INCORRECT to say that war or any other violent behaviour is genetically programmed into our human nature. While genes are involved at all levels of nervous system function, they provide a developmental potential that can be actualised only in conjunction with the ecological and social environment. While individuals vary in their predispositions to be affected by their experience, it is the interaction between their genetic endowment and conditions of nurturance that determines their personalities. Except for rare pathologies, the genes do not produce individuals necessarily predisposed to violence. Neither do they determine the opposite. While genes are co-involved in establishing our behavioural capacities, they do not by themselves specify the outcome.

Third Proposition

IT IS SCIENTIFICALLY INCORRECT to say that in the course of human evolution there has been a selection for aggressive behaviour more than for other kinds of behaviour. In all well-studied species, status within the group is achieved by the ability to co-operate and to fulfill social functions relevant to the structure of that group. 'Dominance' involves social bondings and affiliations; it is not simply a matter of the possession and use of superior physical power, although it does involve aggressive behaviours. Where genetic selection for aggressive behaviour has been artificially instituted in animals, it has rapidly succeeded in producing hyper-aggressive individuals; this indicates that aggression was not maximally selected under natural conditions. When such experimentally-created hyperaggressive animals are present in a social group, they either disrupt its social structure or are driven out. Violence is neither in our evolutionary legacy nor in our genes.

Fourth Proposition

IT IS SCIENTIFICALLY INCORRECT to say that humans have a "violent brain." While we do have the neural apparatus to act violently, it is not automatically activated by internal or external stimuli. Like higher primates and unlike other animals, our higher neural processes filter such stimuli before they can be acted upon. How we act is shaped by how we have been conditioned and socialised. There is nothing in our neurophysiology that compels us to react violently.

Fifth Proposition

IT IS SCIENTIFICALLY INCORRECT to say that war is caused by "instinct" or any single motivation. The emergence of modern warfare has been a journey from the primacy of emotional and motivational factors, sometimes called "instincts," to the primacy of cognitive factors. Modern war involves institutional use of personal characteristics such as obedience, suggestibility, and idealism, social skills such as language, and rational considerations such as cost-calculation, planning, and information processing. The technology of modern war has exaggerated traits associated with violence both in the training of actual combatants and in the preparation of support for war in the general population. As a result of this exaggeration, such traits are often mistaken to be the causes rather than the consequences of the process.

Conclusion

We conclude that biology does not condemn humanity to war, and that humanity can be freed from the bondage of biological pessimism and empowered with confidence to undertake the transformative tasks needed in this International Year of Peace and in the years to come. Although these tasks are mainly institutional and collective, they also rest upon the consciousness of individual participants for whom pessimism and optimism are crucial factors. Just as "wars begin in the minds of men," peace also begins in our minds. The same species who invented war is capable of inventing peace. The responsibility lies with each of us.

Signatories:
- David Adams, Psychology, Wesleyan University, Middletown, Connecticut, U.S.A.
- S.A. Barnett, Ethology, The Australian National University, Canberra, Australia
- N.P. Bechtereva, Neurophysiology, Institute for Experimental Medicine of the Academy of Medical Sciences of the U.S.S.R., Leningrad, U.S.S.R.
- Bonnie Frank Carter, Psychology, Albert Einstein Medical Center, Philadelphia, U.S.A.
- José M. Rodriguez Delgado, Neurophysiology, Centro de Estudios Neurobiológicos, Madrid, Spain
- José Luis Díaz, Ethology, Instituto Mexicano de Psiquiatría, México D.F., Mexico
- Andrzej Eliasz, Individual Differences Psychology, Polish Academy of Sciences, Warsaw, Poland
- Santiago Genovés, Biological Anthropology, Instituto de Estudios Antropológicos, México D.F., Mexico
- Benson E. Ginsburg, Behavior Genetics, University of Connecticut, Storrs, Connecticut, U.S.A.
- Jo Groebel, Social Psychology, Erziehungswissenschaftliche Hochschule, Landau, Federal Republic of Germany
- Samir-Kumar Ghosh, Sociology, Indian Institute of Human Sciences, Calcutta, India
- Robert Hinde, Animal Behaviour, Cambridge University, Cambridge, U.K.
- Richard E. Leakey, Physical Anthropology, National Museums of Kenya, Nairobi, Kenya

- Taha H. Malasi, Psychiatry, Kuwait University, Kuwait
- J. Martín Ramírez, Psychobiology, Universidad de Sevilla, Spain
- Federico Mayor Zaragoza, Biochemistry, Universidad Autónoma, Madrid, Spain
- Diana L. Mendoza, Ethology, Universidad de Sevilla, Spain
- Ashis Nandy, Political Psychology, Centre for the Study of Developing Societies, Delhi, India
- John Paul Scott (geneticist), Animal Behaviour, Bowling Green State University, Bowling Green, Ohio, U.S.A.
- Riitta Wahlstrom, Psychology, University of Jyväskylä, Finland

RESEARCH FINDINGS UPHOLD THE SEVILLE STATEMENT

There is a common slogan, "If you want peace, work for justice." As it turns out, this is a valid formula, according to social science and well-informed observation. Toward the end of one of my trips to Sri Lanka, I was told by a thoughtful young adult that the basis for the long civil war in that country had been unfairness. There was not a fair distribution of power, land, goods, or education. In the case of Sri Lanka, that unfairness led to a 26-year civil war that included terrorist actions, disappearances of many Tamil people, and mayhem. Many who have studied ethnic and religious conflict, myself included, believe that most of the conflicts that seem to be fought along ethnic or religious lines are actually conflicts generated by unfair distribution of power and resources. The sides to these conflicts sometimes break down along religious or ethnic lines, partly due to the geographic distribution of people of these groups. They therefore look like religious or ethnic wars, and are often described as such—perhaps in part to make the motives seem more acceptable and noble, and to help with recruitment of young, idealistic soldiers, but at the end of the day, most of the so-called ethnic and religious conflicts reflect inequitable distribution and/or violations of human rights. And most terrorism is also associated with situations that violate human rights. That is, people of different religions, ethnicities, races, and languages can live together in peace if goods are distributed fairly and human rights are respected.

Social science researchers Alan Krueger and Jitka Maleckova conclude that what they call "political conditions," including lack of civil rights and "longstanding feelings of indignity and frustration" are more likely to predict involvement with terrorism than are poverty or lack of education."[25] This is what social scientists refer to as "grievances" and sometimes "legitimate grievances." These conditions are similar to those that Kenneth Hardy and Tracey Laszloffy describe as conditions fostering violence in teenagers in the United States. In their book *Teens Who Hurt*, they describe adolescents who would rather risk death than be disrespected, with the phrase "death before dis."[26] It is useful to recognize that in some cultures indignity is worse than poverty, and worse than death itself, possibly contributing to the acceptance of planned death in a terrorist attack. Indeed, even in prison systems, as James Gilligan and his colleagues learned, if rights and persons are granted respect, violence and conflict are measurably reduced.[27]

Sociologists Martin Daly and Margo Wilson, in their carefully researched and documented study of homicide over time and across a wide range of geographic and cultural variations, conclude, "There are social milieus where killing is exceedingly rare. With the elimination of social inequity and desperation, we may yet see homicide become an almost negligible source of human mortality."[28] As leaders gathered larger and larger groups under their power and responsibility, revenge gradually became a matter for the larger group, rather than for the family. This further enabled justice to end with one punishment meted out by the state, rather than continuing over generations of revenge. Thus, the establishment of coordinated societies helped to diminish the incidence of violence and homicide.

DEVELOPMENT OF SOCIETIES REDUCES VIOLENCE

Besides ending inequity, Daly and Wilson, in their research, noted another trend in the reduction of violence that is important for our consideration. Historically, a part of the ideology of many stateless societies was that all killings must be avenged. "Early legal codes are largely—sometimes entirely—concerned with the specification of homicide debts."[29] The existence of one strong leader of a large group moves violence from an assault against a family to an assault against the group and its leaders. Thus the leader metes out justice. Developmental scientist Michael Commons and colleagues have applied developmental principles to societies, and their findings lend further support to the idea that the development of societies, which parallels the development of individuals, leads to greater stability and less violence, but only if the societies develop through a series of stages. They offer contemporary and compelling evidence that when societies skip stages, or are encouraged to develop to more sophisticated structures, such as democracy, before having prepared for it, they are likely to fail, with failure including increases in violence and terrorism. It is likely, it seems, that abuses in the areas of human rights are a moderating variable in these societal failures.[30] This view of things might suggest that there was a grain of truth in Thomas Hobbs's assertion that, left to its natural state, without society to tame it, human nature would lead to the life of humans being "solitary, poor, nasty, brutish, and short."[31]

21st-CENTURY SCHOLARSHIP: DEBUNKING MYTHS, PROVIDING EVIDENCE, AND FOSTERING EDUCATION

Twenty-first century scholarship refutes, in very powerful terms, the myths that we are naturally violent and that we are becoming only more violent over time. Indeed, this recent scholarship suggests we may need to improve on our teaching and learning about human history. Both Steven Pinker and Agustín Fuentes, quoted at the start of this chapter, use logic and empirical evidence to indicate conclusively that human nature is evolving toward greater peacefulness and less violence, and not the other way around. In spite of World Wars and terrorism, and in spite of the media coverage and portrayal of violence, humans have become less, not more, violent over time. Our daily lives are not violent. Our wars are not more deadly.

Steven Pinker points out that we have a habit of idealizing and romanticizing the past, including the medieval years. He reminds us that torture of humans was once considered appropriate entertainment, for example, and that humans did not always have a reaction of horror at the thought. Pinker suggests we remember the Age of Reason in the 17th century and the Age of Enlightenment in the 18th century, as these together were times of change. "Medieval Christendom," he reminds us, "was a culture of cruelty."[32]

OBSTACLES TO DEBUNKING THE MYTH THAT HUMANS ARE NATURALLY AGGRESSIVE

Contemporary scientists J. Martin Ramirez, Steven Pinker, and Agustín Fuentes, quoted earlier at the beginning of this chapter, debunk the belief that humans are hopelessly hard-wired for violence and war. It is, simply, scientifically incorrect. What obstacles might be faced in attempting to convince members of the human society of this? Despite logic and evidence, provided in abundance by these scientists, many in society will have been influenced by violence they have witnessed, and small- and large-scale violence they have heard about in society: wars, genocide, tribal warfare, revenge killing, and so on. These do get a lot of attention, both because we as humans are more influenced by the drama of violence and bad outcomes than we are by everyday experiences of peace, love, altruism, care, and responsibility. Besides, violence gets more press. And violence in movies sells tickets.

STRUCTURAL VIOLENCE

Structural violence—violence that is built into our society in such forms as inequality, violations of human rights, dramatic reductions in social safety net programs accompanying increases in wealth disparity, unfairness, prejudice, and so on—may be thought of as the kindling that can lead to physical violence. This has been noticed by scientists, politicians, and common people for centuries. It has led to revolutions, as it did in the American colonies in 1775. Indeed, it might be better said that the perception of structural violence can begin a chain of events that ultimately leads to violence.

How does this apply to young terrorists like the accused bombers Dzhokhar and Tamerlan Tsarnaev? Dzhokhar's tweets and the messages he wrote inside the boat in Watertown, Massachusetts, indicate that his perception was that Americans were unfairly killing Muslims. As discussed in earlier chapters, Dzhokhar was, as a Third Culture Kid and as a young adult, understandably looking to define his loyalties and identities. Predictably, when there is conflict between the country to which one immigrates and some other group to which one feels loyalty—in this case, Muslims—it makes the process more complicated. Leaving Cambridge and the somewhat protected roles of high school student, wrestling team captain, and Cambridge kid, Dzhokhar faced a difficult set of tasks. With his family facing problems, including divorce, legal issues, serious health concerns of his father, loss of food stamps, loss of the apartment where they had lived for many years, departure of both parents to live thousands of miles away, and his brother having lost what was seen as his most likely path to success, Dzhokhar must not have seen the United States as a very hospitable place. While these facts do not excuse his engaging in violence—nothing does—they may help us understand how to prevent other youth like him from being easy targets for recruiters seeking youth to fight in what they convince the youth is a "holy war."

Besides the personal woes—failures and seemingly insurmountable challenges—faced by the Tsarnaevs, it also seems, from news reports about Tamerlan and Zubeidat Tsarnaev, that they—and possibly Dzhokhar—believed that Muslims were unfairly accused in the September 11 bombings. While most news reports suggest that this is strong evidence that the family was disturbed, impaired, or troubled, it is important to note that they were not alone in this belief. Many Americans believe that the American government was somehow deceitful in its reporting on the events of September 11, 2001.[33] There is also, among Arabs and Muslims around the world, a fairly widespread perception that actions of the U.S. government that, if not deliberately targeting Muslims, at least resulted in violence toward Arabs and Muslims and those perceived to be Arab or Muslim. Indeed, just after September 11, 2001, there was a general suspicion and rejection of all immigrants. And it became much more difficult for international students to travel to and from the United States.

This pathway, from the perception of unfairness and structural violence to the reality of politically/religiously motivated violence, with encouragement from recruiters, is one way to understand the connection between injustice and violence.

ONGOING DEVELOPMENTS IN THE REDUCTION OF VIOLENCE: EDUCATION, HUMAN RIGHTS, AND DIPLOMACY

In the final chapter of the 2014 work *Conflict, Violence, Terrorism, and Their Prevention* (edited by J. Martin Ramirez, Chas Morrison, and Arthur J. Kendall), Ramirez, one of the signatories to the Seville Statement, shares his thoughts on promoting peace.[34] Consistent with the science of the 21st century that we have reviewed here, Ramirez emphasizes human rights, education, and expanding peoples' perception of the in-group to include all of society. He goes on to suggest:

I would also like to stress the importance of adequate training in preventive diplomacy for resolution of conflict between states. We need outstanding peacemakers to help resolve disputes in the world. Peacemakers must remember that successful politics is not about finding people who agree with you. It is about making difficult decisions without killing each other. Dialogue is the only way to peace.[35]

This sentiment echoes the Nobel Prize Commission's statement on granting the prize to President Obama in 2009.

Obama has as President created a new climate in international politics. Multilateral diplomacy has regained a central position, with emphasis on the role that the United Nations and other international institutions can play. Dialogue and negotiations are preferred as instruments for resolving even the most difficult international conflicts. The vision of a world free from nuclear arms has powerfully stimulated disarmament and arms control negotiations.[36]

In an earlier work that I coauthored with Samuel J. Sinclair, we also stressed the importance of diplomacy, and provided, as an example, the establishment of the Good Friday agreement in Northern Ireland.

NORTHERN IRELAND

A very instructive, contemporary model of diplomacy leading to a complex, multitiered solution to an ongoing ethnic and religious conflict is the resolution of the situation in Northern Ireland. After years of hatred and violence, even those who hated one another began to see that a negotiated, diplomatic, multiparty solution was desirable. They were not immediately hailed by their parties as heroes. In a chronology posted on PBS Frontline website, there is a note from October 13, 1997, saying:

> British Prime Minister Tony Blair meets with a Sinn Fein delegation and shakes hands with Martin McGuinness and Gerry Adams in East Belfast. Northern Ireland's Protestant majority are outraged, citing the IRA's history of violence and continued unwillingness to lay down their weapons.[37]

But they shouldered on, for a very long time, and in the end a settlement was reached. Ten years later, it is holding, with an ongoing and evidently rather vigorous monitoring process. The United States did assist with this negotiated settlement, and former senator George Mitchell is widely credited as having had an essential role in the creation of the "Good Friday Agreement" reached in Belfast in 1998. The agreement was reached by ongoing negotiations that included terrorist organizations and antiterrorist organizations, and the agreement included early release of some who had been detained for terrorist acts. It may be surprising to realize that, in recent history, various negotiated ceasefires and agreements have included parties accused of terrorism, just as negotiated peace treaties often include parties who had caused harm to one another. Since shortly after September 11, 2001, however, the press and government officials have repeatedly stated that they would not negotiate with terrorists. Such a decision would seem to be at odds with documented breakthroughs in ongoing conflict, all of which have required parties who condemned one another to find the courage to sit down together to create peace. This is not done out of an ideal of love for all or out of an ideal of turning the other cheek. It is not done with blindness to the capacity of the parties for violence, for subterfuge and for sabotage. The brave parties to such talks must be protected from their own enthusiastic group members who see them as traitors. It is done, rather, because it is the only path out of never-ending revenge and violence, the only way for our children and all children to have a chance to be productive and to grow up with hope for a future with opportunity, or for any future at all.[38]

RELEVANCE FOR YOUNG TERRORISTS: ALTRUISM FOR THE GROUP AND AGAINST ADVERSARIES

Wading into the literature on violence throughout history leads quickly to questions that are relevant to recruitment to terrorist organizations today. Whether we are discussing recruitment to the LTTE (recently defunct, but recruiting at least up through a few years ago), or to some Pan-Islamic movement, recruiters seem to be attuned to a pattern that may well be driven by evolution, to an appeal to an altruistic readiness to die for one's family and group, in the context of intergroup conflict. It seems that there is a kind of moral imperative to volunteer for this sort of action that is more powerful than a rational assessment of its impact. Recent findings from scientific research with widely varying cultural groups found that "perceived righteousness but not perceived effectiveness predicted willingness to take part in political violence."[39] This is quite consistent with what we have seen in relation to Dzhokhar Tsarnaev, Hassan Abdi Dhuhulow, and Aymen Saadi, and also consistent with Beate Zschaepe and the un-named Black Tiger, all of whom were considered good kids. None of their actions were likely to have a huge impact, yet they seemingly willingly gave up any chance of a productive life in order to participate in violence that, it is not hard to argue, they saw as being in the service of their loved ones and against the enemies of their loved ones. It is almost as if one is required, by pride, if not by hope, to be willing to be harmed or killed in order to contribute to the possibility that your side will gain and the other will lose.

While initially this finding may seem to diminish hope that violence can be reduced, a second look may suggest possibilities. For example, a body of research in psychology indicates that the relevant definition of one's group is variable, depending on circumstances. That is, one might count those of similar race, gender, or religion as one's in-group in one setting, while, in a different setting one may count others who are fans of the same sports team as members of one's in-group, without regard to any of the variables named earlier. This principle has vastly expanded the size of an in-group from family or small tribe to village or region with the development of leaders of larger groups, and even to patriotism with the development of nations. Is it possible that in some future time this in-group may be all humans?[40] One possible way would be for some common enemy, such as natural disaster or encounters with living beings from one of the millions of planets we now know contain the conditions that would allow life to evolve,[41] could bring people together. But Ramirez speculates that education for peace, that is geared to the developmental level of recipients, could effectively increase the scope of one's perceived in-group to include the entire human race.

The findings of 20th- and 21st-century scientists demonstrate that this possibility is not simply an impossible dream, but a very attainable goal. Indeed, they show us that the human race is already moving in that direction, with help from some very smart, insightful, and caring individuals, including, but surely not limited to, scientists like those of the Pugwash group.

A review of modern history, including genocides and world wars, shows us that it is not only the famous, publicly accomplished individuals who have changed the course of history. Many, many thousands of people whose names we will never know have contributed to the progress of humanity toward reduced violence. Some have taken great risks to move the agenda of human rights forward. But the majority of humans who have contributed to the advance of society toward greater peace and greater regard for human rights have done so in small ways, at moments when they were inspired to perform an action because it simply seemed the right thing to do at the time.

So it seems that the best science of the 21st century has shown that we are not, as humans, doomed by nature to violence. We will not have to settle for lives that are defined by fewer and fewer rights in order to obtain some modicum of safety and security.

Rather, we can focus on enhancing the pace of progress that human society is making toward reducing violence and enhancing human rights. It seems that it is within the capacity of everyone to contribute something toward the reduction of terrorism and other forms of violence and the continued development of a peaceful society.

Some Helpful Books and Articles

These books and articles have been chosen with the goal of helping Americans to better understand the experiences that may have contributed to the bombings at the Boston Marathon. A similar reading list, prepared by someone from another country, or from a religious point of view, would contain, I am sure, different works. I hope these are helpful to readers who want to explore some of the issues raised in this book.

ON YOUTH AND VIOLENCE IN THE UNITED STATES

Some social scientists draw a line between youthful victims and youthful perpetrators of violence, with interest in only one or the other. This has never seemed sensible to me, as the line, it seems to me, is quite permeable. Youth who are immersed in violence, whether as victims, perpetrators, or both, suffer traumatic assaults to their biological, social, and cognitive development. These assaults divert them from a healthy developmental track. There is a range in the degree of resiliency that kids show in response to being immersed in violence. Most do not live lives of violence, though many experiment with violence or aggression, real or considered, as ways to solve problems.

The following books have stood out to me because the authors of these works, too, treat violence as a problem into which some youth are driven or seduced, whether as a victim or perpetrator. There are others, I am sure, but these are the books I would start with.

Canada, Geoffrey. *Fist, Stick, Knife, Gun*. Boston: Beacon Press, 1995.

Canada, Geoffrey. *Reaching Up for Manhood*. Boston: Beacon Press, 1998.

Hardy, Kenneth V., and Tracey A. Laszloffy. *Teens Who Hurt: Clinical Interventions to Break the Cycle of Adolescent Violence*. New York: The Guilford Press, 2006.

Kristof, Nicholas, and Sheryl WuDunn. *Half the Sky: Turning Oppression into Opportunity for Women Worldwide*. New York: Knopf, 2009.

ON CHILD SOLDIERS AND CHILD TERRORISTS AROUND THE WORLD

Some authors' works have been extraordinarily helpful in understanding the world of child soldiers. These books are not easy to read, for sure, but if you want to know what life is like for kids in the real world of conflict and civil war, where the *opposition* wants you dead as soon as possible and your commanders cannot afford to care about you as a person, and where the conditions of fighting make you think those who have died are luckier than those who have survived, these books are a good place to start. A good many child soldiers are recruited to groups that also engage in terrorist activities. There is considerable overlap in the process of getting kids into the militia—whether by kidnapping, threat, or recruitment.

Arnestad, Beate, and Morton Daae. *My Daughter the Terrorist*. Oslo, Norway: Suitt Film Production, 2007.

Beah, Ishmael. *A Long Way Gone: Memoirs of a Boy Soldier*. New York: Sarah Crichton Books, 2007.

Boothby, Neil, Allison Strang, and Michael Wessells. *A World Turned Upside Down: Ecological Approaches to Children in War Zones*. Boulder, CO: Kumarian Press, 2006.

Briggs, Jimmie. *Innocents Lost: When Child Soldiers Go to War*. New York: Basic Books, 2005.

Coomaraswamy, Radhika. "Child Soldiers: Root Causes and UN Initiatives." Seminar, *Center for the Education of Women, University of Michigan, Ann Arbor*, February 2009.

FARC Systematically Recruits Child Soldiers, Published by Colombia Reports, cited by UNHCR Refugees Daily, September 17, 2013, http://www.unhcr.org/cg—bin/texis/vtx/refdaily?pass=463ef21123& id=52393a095.

Human Rights Watch Report on Child Soldiers Worldwide, http://www .hrw.org/node/105699.

LoCicero, Alice, and Samuel J. Sinclair. *Creating Young Martyrs: Conditions That Make Dying in a Terrorist Attack Seem Like a Good Idea.* Westport, CT: Praeger, 2008.

McConnell, Faith J. H., and Grace Akallo. *Girl Soldier: A Story of Hope for Uganda's Children.* Grand Rapids, MI: Baker Publishers, 2007.

Rosen, David. *Armies of the Young: Child Soldiers in War and Terrorism.* New Brunswick, NJ: Rutgers University Press, 2005.

ON IMMIGRATION—NONFICTION

Many Americans whose grandparents or great-grandparents were immigrants are simply not aware of the struggles that immigrants face. The large wave of immigrants who came to the United States in the late 19th and early 20th centuries tried to assimilate as quickly as possible, and talked little about their struggles. In addition, that was a time when people talked a lot less about emotions than they do now. (Freud's "taking cure" had barely been introduced.) Therefore, many will have to be open to learning of the concerns faced by immigrants in the United States today, and will wonder why the older generation did not seem to have such a struggle. They probably did; they just didn't talk about it.

Mahalingam, Ramaswami. *Cultural Psychology of Immigrants.* Mahwah, NJ: Lawrence Erlbaum, 2006.

Pollock, David C., and Ruth E. Van Reken. *Third Culture Kids: Growing Up among Worlds.* Rev. Ed. Boston: Nicholas Brealey Publishing, 2009. Kindle edition.

ON IMMIGRATION—FICTION

Many young immigrants have told me that Lahiri's book captures the sense of the life of a young immigrant quite well.

Lahiri, Jhumpa. *The Namesake: A Novel.* New York: Mariner Books, 2004.

ON TERRORISM

Quite a few social scientists were studying modern terrorism long before September 11, 2001, when it became a topic of interest to many Americans. The following is a list of well-regarded books that I found helpful. It is not an exhaustive list.

Bergen, Peter L. *The Osama bin Laden I Knew.* New York: Free Press, 2006.

Hoffman, Bruce. *Inside Terrorism.* New York: Columbia University Press, 2006.

McCauley, Clark. *Terrorism Research and Public Policy.* London: Routledge, 1991.

Moghaddam, Fathali. *From the Terrorists' Point of View.* Westport, CT: Praeger, 2006.

Pyszczynski, Thomas A., Sheldon Solomon, and Jeff Greenberg. *In the Wake of 9–11: The Psychology of Terror.* Washington, DC: American Psychological Association, 2003.

Ramirez, J. Martin, Chas Morrison, and Arthur J. Kendall. *Conflict, Violence, Terrorism, and Their Prevention.* Newcastle upon Tyne: Cambridge Scholars, 2014.

Richardson, Louise. *What Terrorists Want: Understanding the Enemy, Containing the Threat.* New York: Random House, 2007.

Stern, Jessica. *Terror in the Name of God: Why Religious Militants Kill.* New York: Harper, 2004.

ON COUNTERTERRORISM

While most of us would prefer to live in a world without terrorism, it has become clear over time that some of the attempts to keep Americans safe and to combat terrorism have had costs to society, and sometimes the costs seem to outweigh the benefits. Here are just two of many publications that address the cost of efforts to combat terrorism. The first, *Collateral Damage*, consists of essays that cover a wide range of areas where counterterrorism efforts have led to difficulties.

Kimmel, Paul, and Chris E. Stout, *Collateral Damage: The Psychological Consequences of America's War on Terrorism.* Westport, CT: Praeger, 2006.

Suskind, Ron. *The One Percent Doctrine.* New York: Simon and Schuster, 2007.

FICTION THAT ILLUMINATES TERRORISM

One of the most highly regarded social scientists, Erik Erikson, often used fiction to illustrate psychological theory. The following works provide a deep insight, in my opinion, into the minds and hearts of young terrorists, and young people who resist terrorism. The book by Updike, especially, captures the process of recruitment of a young, devout Muslim to perform a terrorist action in which he plans to die. Works by Jones and

Patchett show the very human side of young people viewing terrorism. In Jones's book, a flash of insight leads a young man to reject terrorism. And Soans's play is based on actual quotes, and argues strongly for the sort of conversation that Thich Naht Hanh recommends, to help remove wrong perceptions. Malraux's book, hard to read because of the violence, is recommended as a means of insight into the motivation of a young terrorist, and the process of socialization to a terrorist's viewpoint.

Jones, Marie. *A November Night*. London: Nick Hern Books, 2000.
Malraux, Andre. *Man's Fate*. New York: Modern Library, 1934.
Patchett, Ann. *Bel Canto*. New York, NY: HarperCollins, 2002.
Soans, Robin. *Talking to Terrorists*. London: Oberon Books, 2006.
Updike, John. *Terrorist*. New York: Ballantine Books, 2006.

ON REACHING FOR MUTUAL UNDERSTANDING AND NONVIOLENCE

A great deal has been written about dialogue, and about reaching across differences for mutual understanding. The book *Difficult Conversations* is a kind of how-to for everyday conversations where one has to work to understand the other person's point of view. I have recommended it many times and have found that most people see it as very useful. I also include a set of films by the group Just Vision. These films are about comrades across the Israel-Palestine divide. In each film, we see how hard it is to see the "other's" point of view, yet we also see some of the most unexpected collaborations and mutual support. This inspires us to consider why, if such unlikely people can reach across the divide, it is so hard for their leaders to do so.

Just Vision Films. *Encounter Point* (2007), *Budrus* (2011), *My Neighborhood* (2012), and *Homefront* (2013).
Stone, Douglas, Bruce Patton, and Sheila Heen. *Difficult Conversations*. New York: Penguin, 2010.

ON THE ACCUSED BOSTON MARATHON BOMBERS

Hundreds of articles have been written, many of them within days of the Boston Marathon bombing, and each making some contribution to understanding the life and experiences of the bombers. The following two articles seem to me to be most complete and compelling. The first article was mostly ignored in the controversy about the cover of *The Rolling Stones* magazine. That is unfortunate, because the article itself is a good one. The second article emphasizes family pathology, and is harsh in its criticism of the Tsarnaev family. I think it goes too far, and reflects less awareness of cultural difference and of issues common to immigrants. However, it does contain some helpful information.

Jacobs, Sally, David Filipov, and Patricia Wen. "Fall of the House of Tsarnaev." *Boston Globe*, December 15, 2013. http://www.bostonglobe .com/Page/Boston/2011-2020/WebGraphics/Metro/BostonGlobe .com/2013/12/15tsarnaev/tsarnaev.html
Reitman, Janet. "Jahar's World." *Rolling Stone*, August 1, 2013. http:// www.rollingstone.com/culture/news/jahars-world-20130717

ON VIOLENCE AND HUMAN NATURE

Fuentes, Agustin. *Race, Monogamy, and Other Lies They Told You: Busting Myths about Human Nature*. Berkeley: University of California Press, 2012. Kindle edition.
Pinker, Steven. *The Better Angels of Our Nature: Why Violence Has Declined*. London: Penguin Group, 2011. Kindle edition.
Ramirez, J. Martin. "Moving toward Peace." In *Conflict, Violence, Terrorism, and Their Prevention*, edited by J. M. Ramirez, C. Morrison, and A. J. Kendall. Newcastle upon Tyne, UK: Cambridge Scholars Publishing, 2014.

ON CHECHNYA AND THE CAUCASUS

As I struggled to grasp the magnitude of the difficulties in Chechnya over hundreds of years, the following books, among many readings, stood out as helping me to get a sense of the experience of living in the context of unrelenting violence and war, with neither side in the conflict being trustworthy, and with death and trauma commonplace.

Baiev, Khassan, and Ruth Daniloff. *The Oath: A Surgeon under Fire*. New York: Walker Publishing Company, 2004.
Politkovskaya, Anna. *A Small Corner of Hell: Dispatches from Chechnya*. Translated by Alexander Burry and Tatiana Tulchinsky. Chicago: University of Chicago Press, 2007. Kindle edition.
Solzhenitsyn, Aleksandr I. *The Gulag Archipelago*. New York: Harper and Row 1973.

ON ISLAM

The following three-part series on the *Life of Muhammed* was very helpful to me in increasing the depth of my understanding of the origins of the faith, and the great respect with which Muslims hold Muhammed.

Faris Kermani, Producer and Director. *The Life of Muhammed*. London: Crescent Films for the BBC, 2011.

Notes

INTRODUCTION

1. The White House, "Statement by the President," April 19, 2013, http://www.whitehouse.gov/the-press-office/2013/04/19/statement-president.

2. The author's advance is being contributed to the One Fund.

3. Journalist Anna Politskovskaya, author of a work about Chechnyans' daily life during conflict, published in 2003, called *A Small Corner of Hell*, was killed at her Moscow apartment building in 2006. Her work revealed abuses of human rights, and her killers have not been brought to justice. The U.S. State Department issued the following statement in October 2013: "Anna Politkovskaya's reporting on the war in the North Caucasus region brought to light the violation of human rights and the suffering of the victims in this conflict. Her unsolved murder, and that of other journalists, including Paul Klebnikov, Akhmednabi Akhmednabiyev, Kazbek Gakkiyev, and several others in the North Caucasus in recent years, has created an atmosphere of intimidation for those who work to uncover corruption or human rights abuses." See "Seven Year Anniversary of the Murder of Anna Politkovskaya," U.S. Department of State Press Statement, October 7, 2013, http://www.state.gov/r/pa/prs/ps/2013/10/215185.htm.

4. International Crisis Group, The North Caucasus: The Challenges of Integration (III), Governance, Elections, *Rule of Law*. September 2013

Report, http://www.crisisgroup.org/en/regions/europe/north-caucasus/226-north-caucasus-the-challenges-of-integration-iii-governance-elections-rule-of-law.aspx.

CHAPTER 1

1. Cambridge Public Schools, *Student Data Report School Year 2009–2010*, http://www3.cpsd.us/media/theme/Pro-Cambridge/network/10516/media/CPS%20Redesign/documents/SAA/Student_Data_Reports/SDR_%202009-10.pdf?rev=0.

2. Janet Reitman, "Jahar's World," *Rolling Stone*, August 1, 2013, http://www.rollingstone.com/culture/news/jahars-world-20130717.

3. They were also accused of the murder of MIT police officer Sean Collier, and the ensuing chaotic attempts to escape, including carjacking and attempts to harm local and state police in a melee that took place in Watertown, Massachusetts.

4. Reitman, "Jahar's World."

5. Ibid.

6. Joan Micklin Silver, *Hester Street* (Midwest Films, 1975), DVD.

7. Reitman, "Jahar's World."

8. Alice LoCicero and Samuel J. Sinclair, *Creating Young Martyrs: Conditions That Make Dying in a Terrorist Attack Seem Like a Good Idea* (Contemporary Psychology, 2008), 41.

9. Reitman, "Jahar's World."

10. Gavin Aronsen, "Wrestling Photo, Stunned Reactions from Former Classmates of Bombing Suspect Dzhokhar Tsarnaev," *Mother Jones*, April 19, 2013, http://www.motherjones.com/print/222656.

11. Jon Cohen, "Most Want Death Penalty for Dzhokhar Tsarnaev If He Is Convicted of Boston Bombing," *Washington Post*, May 1, 2013, http://articles.washingtonpost.com/2013-05-01/world/38940946_1_death-penalty-whites-35-percent.

12. Abby Ohlheiser, "Most Boston Residents Wouldn't Give Dzhokhar Tsarnaev the Death Penalty," *The Atlantic Wire*, September 16, 2013, http://www.theatlanticwire.com/national/2013/09/boston-residents-wouldnt-give-dzhokhar-tsarnaev-death-penalty/69468/.

13. Jeffrey M. Jones, "U.S. Death Penalty Support Lowest in More Than 40 Years," *Gallup*, October 29, 2013, http://www.gallup.com/poll/165626/death-penalty-support-lowest-years.aspx.

14. Fathali Moghaddam, *From the Terrorists' Point of View* (Westport, CT: Praeger, 2006).

15. Controversy over the Supreme Court 2010 ruling in the case *Holder v. Humanitarian Law Project* is reflective of the unsettled question as to how to influence organizations that engage in terrorist activities. The judgment seems, to some, to be justifiable and to increase the security of the United States. To others, it seems to have the potential to interfere with activities that could reduce terrorism.

16. Accomplished experts on the study of terrorism, such as Clark McCauley, argue that terrorist movements would actively exclude anyone who showed signs of being insane. This is because members of terrorist groups depend on one another in order to carry out a planned attack. They would not want someone whose sense of reality was compromised, or whose emotions interfered with their ability to act according to a plan, because they depend on each team member to do his or her part as agreed upon. So far as has been revealed to the public as of this time it does not seem likely that the Tsarnaev brothers were directly supported by an organization, and some have suggested that the older brother may have had some mental health concerns. However, if he did have some difficulties, they did not seem to interfere with his ability to plan and carry out the attack. The actions of the Tsarnaev brothers after the release o their photos do not appear to have been planned in advance.

17. Audrey Kurth Cronin, *How Terrorism Ends* (Princeton, NJ: Princeton University Press, 2009).

18. Ibid.

19. Robert H. Jackson, *Opening Statement before the International Military Tribunal*, 1945, http://www.roberthjackson.org/the-man/speeches-articles /speeches/speeches-by-robert-h-jackson/opening-statement-before-the-international-military-tribunal/.

TIMELINE

1. Jonathan Riley-Smith, *The Crusades, Christianity, and Islam (Bampton Lectures in America)* (New York: Columbia University Press, 2008), Kindle Edition, 5.

2. "Tamerlane," The Applied History Research Group, The University of Calgary, 2000, http://www.ucalgary.ca/appplied_history/tutor/old wrld/armies/tamerlane.html.

3. "Chronology of Chechens in Russia," Center for International Development and Conflict Management, University of Maryland, 2010, http://www.cidcm.umd.edu/mar/chronology.asp?groupId=36504.

4. Ibid.

5. Ibid.

6. "Palestinian-Israeli Conflict," Arizona Military Museum, http://www.azdema.gov/museum/famousbattles/pdf/Palestinian-Israeli%20Conflict-072809.pdf.

7. Sally Jacobs, David Filipov, and Patricia Wen, "The Fall of the House of Tsarnaev," *Boston Globe*, December 15, 2013, http://www.bostonglobe.com/Page/Boston/2011-2020/WebGraphics/Metro/Boston-Globe.com/2013/12/15tsarnaev/tsarnaev.html.

8. Marc Fisher, "The Tsarnaev Family: A Faded Portrait of an Immigrant's American Dream," *Washington Post*, April 27, 2013, http://www.washingtonpost.com/sf/feature/wp/2013/04/27/the-tsarnaev-family-a-faded-portrait-of-an-immigrants-american-dream/.

9. "Establishment of Israel," Jewish Virtual Library, http://www.jewishvirtuallibrary.org/jsource/History/Dec_of_Indep.html.

10. "Chronology," Center for International Development and Conflict Management.

11. Tom Parfitt, "Boston Bombers' Father to Travel to US to Bury Tamerlan Tsarnaev," *Telegraph*, April 25, 2013, http://www.telegraph.co.uk/news/worldnews/northamerica/usa/10019201/Boston-bombers-father-to-travel-to-US-to-bury-Tamerlan-Tsarnaev.html.

12. Alan Cullison, Paul Sonne, Anton Troianovski, and David George-Cosh, "Turn to Religion Splits Suspects' Home," *Wall Street Journal*, April 22, 2013, http://online.wsj.com/news/articles/SB10001424127278Cull87324235304578437131250259170.

13. "Chronology," Center for International Development and Conflict Management.

14. Reitman, "Jahar's World."

15. Ibid.

16. Deborah Sontag, David Herszenhorn, and Serge F. Kovaleski, "A Battered Dream, Then a Violent Path," *New York Times*, April 27, 2013, http://www.nytimes.com/2013/04/28/us/shot-at-boxing-title-denied-tamerlan-tsarnaev-reeled.html?_r=0.

17. Jacobs, Filipov, and Wen, "The Fall of the House of Tsarnaev."

18. "Chronology," Center for International Development and Conflict Management.

19. Kim Murphy, Joseph Tanfani, and Sergei L. Loiko, "The Tsarnaev Brothers' Troubled Trail to Boston," *Los Angeles Times*, April 28, 2013, http://www.latimes.com/news/nationworld/nation/la-na-boston-suspects-20130428-dto,0,15030.htmlstory#axzz2l1NGQoaH. See also Jacobs, Filipov, and Wen, "The Fall of the House of Tsarnaev."

20. Reitman, "Jahar's World."

21. Ibid.

22. "Chronology," Center for International Development and Conflict Management.

23. Ibid.

24. Khassan Baiev and Ruth Daniloff, *The Oath: A Surgeon under Fire* (New York: Walker Publishing Company, 2004).

25. "Norway Tried to Stop Hassan Abdi Dhuhulow, One of Westgate Mall Attackers," *Epoch Times*, October 23, 2013, http://www.theepoch times.com/n3/327184-norway-tried-to-stop-hassan-abdi-dhuhulow-one-of-westgate-mall-attackers/.

26. "Chronology," Center for International Development and Conflict Management.

27. Cullison, Sonne, Troianovski, and George-Cosh, "Turn to Religion Splits Suspects' Home."

28. Christian Caryl, "The Bombers World," *New York Review of Books*, June 6, 2013, http://www.nybooks.com/articles/archives/2013/jun/06/bombers-world/.

29. Murphy, Tanfani, and Loiko, "The Tsarnaev Brothers' Troubled Trail to Boston."

30. Sontag, Herszenhorn, and Kovaleski, "A Battered Dream, Then a Violent Path."

31. Jacobs, Filipov, and Wen, "The Fall of the House of Tsarnaev." Tamerlan and Dzhokhar, children at this time, would likely have been affected, perhaps traumatized, by these events.

32. "Timeline: A Look at Tamerlan Tsarnaev's Past," *CNN*, April 22, 2013, http://www.cnn.com/2013/04/21/us/tamerlan-tsarnaev-timeline/.

33. Peter Ford, "Europe Cringes at Bush 'Crusade' against Terrorists," *Christian Science Monitor*, September 19, 2001, http://www.csmonitor.com/2001/0919/p12s2-woeu.html.

34. Fisher, "The Tsarnaev Family."

35. Aronsen, "Wrestling Photo, Stunned Reactions from Former Classmates of Bombing Suspect Dzhokhar Tsarnaev." See also Jacobs, Filipov, and Wen, "The Fall of the House of Tsarnaev."

36. Chris Cassidy, "Tsarnaev Family Received $100G in Benefits," *Boston Herald*, April 29, 2013, http://bostonherald.com/news_opinion/local_coverage/2013/04/tsarnaev_family_received_100g_in_benefits

37. Jacobs, Filipov, and Wen, "The Fall of the House of Tsarnaev."

38. "Timeline: A Look at Tamerlan Tsarnaev's Past," *CNN*.

39. Ibid.

40. Jacobs, Filipov and Wen, "The Fall of the House of Tsarnaev."

41. Ibid.

42. Amy Saltzman, "Slain Bombing Suspect Had Arrest Record in Cambridge," *Wicked Local Cambridge*, April 20, 2013, http://www .wickedlocal.com/cambridge/news/x1148865564/Slain-bombing-suspect-had-arrest-record-in-Cambridge#.

43. Reitman, "Jahar's World."

44. "Timeline: A Look at Tamerlan Tsarnaev's Past," *CNN*.

45. Fisher, "The Tsarnaev Family."

46. Sontag, Herszenhorn, and Kovaleski, "A Battered Dream, Then a Violent Path."

47. "Timeline: A Look at Tamerlan Tsarnaev's Past," *CNN*.

48. Jacobs, Filipov, and Wen, "The Fall of the House of Tsarnaev."

49. Ibid.

50. "Chronology," Center for International Development and Conflict Management.

51. Sebastian Rotella, "Boston Bombing Suspects Echo Home-Grown Terrorists in Madrid, London Attacks," *Propublica*, April 20, 2013, http:// www.propublica.org/article/boston-bombing-suspects-echo-home-grown-terrorists-in-madrid-london-att.

52. Julie Bycowizc, "Tamerlan Tsarnaev's Family Crumbled before Boston Bombs," *Bloomberg*, April 23, 2013, http://www.bloomberg.com /news/2013–04–23/mom-shoplifts-as-her-boys-become-radicalized.html.

53. "Timeline: A Look at Tamerlan Tsarnaev's Past," *CNN*.

54. Alan Cullison, Paul Sonne and Jennifer Levits, "Life in America Unraveled for Brothers," *Wall Street Journal*, April 20, 2013, http://online.wsj .com/news/articles/SB10001424127887323809304578432501435232278.

55. Murphy, Tanfani, and Loiko, "The Tsarnaev Brothers' Troubled Trail to Boston."

56. Jacobs, Filipov, and Wen, "The Fall of the House of Tsarnaev." Post-hoc and postmortem speculation included in this article suggests the possibility that the voice or voices may have reflected serious mental illness. The article indicates that no psychiatric treatment was received by Tamerlan.

57. "Timeline: A Look at Tamerlan Tsarnaev's Past," *CNN*.

58. Cullison, Sonne, Troianovski, and George-Cosh, "Turn to Religion Splits Suspects' Home."

59. Oren Dorell, "Boston Suspects' Mosque Has Ties to Convicted Terrorists, Fugitives and Radical Speakers," *USA Today*, April 23, 2013, http://www.usatoday.com/story/news/nation/2013/04/23/boston-mosque-radicals/2101411/.

60. Jon Swaine, "Tamerlan Tsarnaev's Wife Katherine Russell Wore the Hijab after Converting to Islam," *Telegraph*, April 20, 2013, http:// www.telegraph.co.uk/news/worldnews/northamerica/usa/10007326

/Tamerlan-Tsarnaevs-wife-Katherine-Russell-wore-the-hijab-after-converting-to-Islam.html.

61. Jacobs, Filipov, and Wen, "The Fall of the House of Tsarnaev."

62. Ibid.

63. "Norway Tried to Stop Hassan Abdi Dhuhulow," *Epoch Times.*

64. Kirit Radia, "Bomb Suspects' Mother Says Young Son Would Have Obeyed Older Brother," Good Morning America, *ABC News*, April 22, 2013, http://abcnews.go.com/International/boston-bomb-suspects-mother-young-son-obeyed-big/story?id=19014490.

65. Reitman, "Jahar's World."

66. Ibid.

67. "Timeline: A Look at Tamerlan Tsarnaev's Past," *CNN.*

68. Fisher, "The Tsarnaev Family."

69. Sontag, Herszenhorn, and Kovaleski, "A Battered Dream, Then a Violent Path."

70. Ibid.

71. Jacobs, Filipov, and Wen, "The Fall of the House of Tsarnaev." This next instance of their father being beaten would be expected to have an impact on Dzhokhar and Tamerlan, perhaps more so due to the earlier experience of their father's being a victim of violence, together with the violence they likely witnessed when the family fled Chechnya at the start of the unrest and war in the early 1990s.

72. Reitman, "Jahar's World."

73. Ellen Barry, "With Breakdown of Order in Russia's Dagestan Region, Fear Stalks Police," *New York Times*, March 20, 2010, http://www.nytimes .com/2010/03/21/world/europe/21dagestan.html?pagewanted=all. See also Ellen Barry, "Dagestan's Shadow War, Fought by 'Many Tsarnaevs,'" *New York Times*, May 19, 2013, http://www.nytimes.com/2013/05/20/world /europe/bomb-suspects-trip-sheds-light-on-caucasus-war.html?_r=0.

74. "Timeline: A Look at Tamerlan Tsarnaev's Past," *CNN.*

75. Reitman, "Jahar's World."

76. "Norway Tried to Stop Hassan Abdi Dhuhulow," *Epoch Times.*

77. Sontag, Herszenhorn, and Kovaleski, "A Battered Dream, Then a Violent Path."

78. Fisher, "The Tsarnaev Family."

79. Multiple sources, including Jacobs, Filipov, and Wen, "The Fall of the House of Tsarnaev."

80. Sontag, Herszenhorn, and Kovaleski, "A Battered Dream, Then a Violent Path."

81. Francis X. Rocca, "Muslim Seminary Ends Talks with Vatican Over Pope's Comments," *Huffington Post*, January 20, 2011, http://www

.huffingtonpost.com/2011/01/20/muslim-seminary-ends-talk_n_811839
.html.

82. Reitman, "Jahar's World."

83. Ibid.

84. Sontag, Herszenhorn, and Kovaleski, "A Battered Dream, Then a
Violent Path."

85. Jacobs, Filipov, and Wen, "The Fall of the House of Tsarnaev."

86. "Timeline: A Look at Tamerlan Tsarnaev's Past," *CNN*.

87. Michael Wines and Ian Lovett, "The Dark Side, Carefully Masked,"
New York Times, May 4, 2013, http://www.nytimes.com/2013/05/05/us
/dzhokhar-tsarnaevs-dark-side-carefully-masked.html.

88. Fisher, "The Tsarnaev Family."

89. Reitman, "Jahar's World."

90. Ibid.

91. Jacobs, Filipov, and Wen, "The Fall of the House of Tsarnaev."

92. Fisher, "The Tsarnaev Family."

93. Jacobs, Filipov, and Wen, "The Fall of the House of Tsarnaev."

94. According to *The Globe* article "The Fall of the House of Tsarnaev," during his visit to Dagestan, Tamerlan spent time with members
of the Union of the Just, a group that campaigns against human rights violations against Muslims. This group, led by a cousin of Tamerlan's, does not
espouse violence. They are critical of the U.S. interventions in Muslim
countries. His companions in Dagestan gave him a second name, "Muaz"
after an Islamic scholar. This name, perhaps, could have been a counterbalance to the name Tamerlan, which was a variation on Timor the Lame,
a Muslim fighter and leader from the 14th century.

95. Jacobs, Filipov, and Wen, "The Fall of the House of Tsarnaev."

96. Tom Hays, "In a Brooklyn Courtroom, Terrorists Testify about
Subway Suicide Plot," *Brooklyn Daily Eagle*, April 16, 2012, http://
www.brooklyneagle.com/articles/brooklyn-courtroom-terrorists-testify-
about-subway-suicide-plot. See also Mosi Secret, "In Terrorists' Testimony, a Rare, Intimate Look into a Secretive World," *New York Times*,
April 29, 2012, http://www.nytimes.com/2012/04/30/nyregion/testimony-
of-4-admitted-terrorists-gives-a-rare-view-of-al-qaeda.html

97. Jacobs, Filipov, and Wen, "The Fall of the House of Tsarnaev."

98. Fisher, "The Tsarnaev Family."

99. "Timeline: A Look at Tamerlan Tsarnaev's Past," *CNN*.

100. Fisher, "The Tsarnaev Family."

101. Sontag, Herszenhorn, and Kovaleski, "A Battered Dream, Then
a Violent Path."

102. Reitman, "Jahar's World."

103. Ibid.

104. Jacobs, Filipov, and Wen, "The Fall of the House of Tsarnaev."

105. "Timeline: A Look at Tamerlan Tsarnaev's Past," *CNN.*

106. Reitman, "Jahar's World."

107. Fisher, "The Tsarnaev Family."

108. "Timeline: A Look at Tamerlan Tsarnaev's Past," *CNN.*

109. Reitman, "Jahar's World."

110. Ibid.

111. "Timeline: A Look at Tamerlan Tsarnaev's Past," *CNN.*

112. Reitman, "Jahar's World."

113. Jacobs, Filipov, and Wen, "The Fall of the House of Tsarnaev."

114. Reitman, "Jahar's World."

115. Ibid.

116. Ibid.

117. Fisher, "The Tsarnaev Family."

118. Reitman, "Jahar's World."

119. Ibid.

120. Ibid.

121. Deborah Kotz, "Injury Toll from Marathon Bombs Reduced to 264," *Boston Globe,* April 24, 2013, http://www.bostonglobe.com/lifestyle/health-wellness/2013/04/23/number-injured-marathon-bombing-revised-downward/NRpaz5mmvGquP7KMA6XsIK/story.html.

122. Ibid.

123. Fisher, "The Tsarnaev Family."

124. Eric Ortiz, "'He Was Just Relaxed': After Attack, Boston Marathon Bombing Suspect Dzhokhar Tsarnaev Partied, Went to Gym," *New York Daily News,* April 20, 2013, http://www.nydailynews.com/news/crime/dzhokhar-tsarnaev-partied-gym-days-bombing-article-1.1322828.

125. Fisher, "The Tsarnaev Family."

126. "Pope Francis' Letter to Grand Imam of Al-Azhar Calls for Mutual Understanding between Christians and Muslims," *Huffington Post,* September 18, 2013, http://www.huffingtonpost.com/2013/09/18/pope-francis-letter-al-azhar_n_3948461.html.

127. "Norway Tried to Stop Hassan Abdi Dhuhulow," *Epoch Times.*

128. Trond Hugubakken, "Norwegian Citizen Possibly Involved in the Terrorist Attack in Kenya," *PST Pressemeldinger,* October 10, 2013, http://www.pst.no/media/pressemeldinger/norwegian-citizen-possibly-involved-in-the-terrorist-attack-in-kenya/.

129. Various reports, including Albina Kovalyova and Alastair Jamieson, "Female Suicide Bomber Suspected of Russia Bus Blast; at least Five Dead," *NBC News,* October 21, 2013, http://worldnews.nbcnews

.com/_news/2013/10/21/21062945-female-suicide-bomber-suspected-of-russia-bus-blast-at-least-5-dead?lite. There were seven deaths, including the bomber, resulting from this blast.

130. Jacobs, Filipov, and Wen correctly raise some concern that evident parental non-engagement, or unreliable engagement, may have been factors contributing to the Tsarnaev brothers' vulnerability, but they tend to disregard the likely impact of recruitment. The article also tends to rely on the memory of friends and neighbors, including some from years back, before the family immigrated, but psychological research has demonstrated that eyewitness accounts, even those for more recent events, are unreliable. Furthermore, the bombings are apt to color the memories of what happened before the bombings. The article also interpreted as problematic some patterns that might have been better explained by poverty, and/or cultural and immigrant status, such as the large, loud family living in what, to middle class, third-, or fourth-generation Americans, would seem to be a small home.

131. Steven Lee Myers, "Bombings Jolt Russia, Raising Olympic Fears," *New York Times*, December 30, 2013, http://www.nytimes.com/2013/12/30/world/europe/volgograd-russia-explosion.html?hpw&rref=world.

132. "Mapping Militant Organizations," *Stanford University*, updated August 9, 2010, http://www.stanford.edu/group/mappingmilitants/cgi-bin/groups/view/255.

133. Milton J. Valencia, *Boston Globe*, http://www.bostonglobe.com/metro/2014/03/28/dzhokhar-tsarnaev-attorneys-seek-government-evidence-tamerlan-say-may-help-defense/PJoDIO3Tdf3zlau7VM9m8L/story.html.

CHAPTER 2

1. Henrik Pryser Libell and Nicholas Kulish, "In Kenya Inquiry, Norway Looks at Somali Migrant," *New York Times*, October 18, 2013, http://www.nytimes.com/2013/10/19/world/africa/norway-suspect-nairobi-kenya-mall-siege.html.

2. Tony Paterson, "Neo-Nazi Nuremberg: Germany Forced to Confront Its Dark Side," *The Independent*, May 3, 2013, http://www.independent.co.uk/news/world/europe/neonazi-nuremberg-germany-forced-to-confront-its-dark-side-8602738.html.

3. Reitman, "Jahar's World."

4. Carlotta Gall, "Worry in Tunisia Over Youths Who Turn to Jihad," *New York Times*, December 18, 2013, http://www.nytimes.com/2013/12/19/world/middleeast/young-tunisians-are-being-recruited-to-jihad.html?_r=0

5. *My Daughter the Terrorist*, directed by Beate Arnestad (The Netherlands: Snit Film Production, 2007), DVD.

6. It is unclear whether this young volunteer Black Tiger actually carried out a terrorist attack prior to the end of the war in Sri Lanka, but it is clear that she had volunteered, and that other young Tigers have carried out attacks in which they, as well as innocent civilians, were killed. It is also true that young Palestinians, viewed as devout and having no history of problems, have been chosen and have carried out similar missions.

7. "How Does a Boy from a Seaside Town in Norway End Up a Terrorist in Kenya?" produced by Joyce Hackel, The World, *PRI*, October 24, 2013, http://www.pri.org/stories/2013-10-24/how-does-boy-seaside-town-norway-end-terrorist-kenya.

8. Carlotta Gall, "Worry in Tunisia Over Youths Who Turn to Jihad," *New York Times*, December 18, 2013, http://www.nytimes.com/2013/12/19/world/middleeast/young-tunisians-are-being-recruited-to-jihad.html?_r=0

9. When Samuel Sinclair and I wrote *Creating Young Martyrs*, based on research with youth in Sri Lanka at risk of recruitment to the Tamil Tigers, we predicted that it was only a matter of time before youth in the United States began to engage in terrorist acts.

10. Norway's population is small (about 5 million, compared with roughly 325 million in the United States) and is 94 percent of Norwegian heritage. These factors come into play in the more individualized approach of Norway's Politiets Sikkerhetstjeneste or PST (Police Security Service, often compared with MI5 in the United Kingdom.) The PST is open about its approach of tracking people who leave Norway to become trained or participate in terrorist organizations. The PST states the following on its website: "We have lately seen an increase in the number of persons leaving Norway to take part in acts of war, attend training camps or join terrorist networks abroad. We are concerned that this development may have an increasingly negative impact on the threat situation in Norway." Hugubakken, "Norwegian Citizen Possibly Involved in the Terrorist Attack in Kenya."

11. The delay in Tamerlan's path to citizenship may have dashed his hopes of success in his boxing career, and may have been one among many factors that led him to turn from working toward success as an American to working toward disrupting American life through terrorist action. It seems unlikely that this challenge alone is the cause of his radicalization, but it is likely one of many factors.

12. Indeed, some believe that he was already a killer before going to Dagestan, as some believe he was involved in a triple murder that took place in Waltham, Massachusetts, in 2011.

13. Hays, "In a Brooklyn Courtroom, Terrorists Testify about Subway Suicide Plot." See also Secret, "In Terrorists' Testimony, a Rare, Intimate Look into a Secretive World."

14. Louise Richardson, *What Terrorists Want: Understanding the Enemy, Containing the Threat* (New York: Random House, 2007), 4.

15. Alice LoCicero and Samuel J. Sinclair, "Terrorism and Terrorist Leaders: Insights from Developmental and Ecological Psychology," *Studies in Conflict and Terrorism* 31, no. 3 (2008): 227–50.

16. The criterion of sanity serves to focus our attention on the fact that, while some heinous acts are committed by people who are not sane, most heinous acts are committed by people who are sane, and people with psychosis are only slightly more likely to be dangerous than people who are sane. Most of the difference is accounted for by people with mental disorders who also abuse drugs or alcohol.

17. LoCicero and Sinclair, "Terrorism and Terrorist Leaders: Insights from Developmental and Ecological Psychology."

18. Charles King. "Not Your Average Chechen Jihadis," *Foreign Affairs*, April 21, 2013, http://www.foreignaffairs.com/articles/139333/charles-king/not-your-average-chechen-jihadis.

19. Richard Brookhiser, "Domestic Terrorism: The Killers Next Door," *American History* 48, no. 4 (2013): 17–18.

20. Khassan Baiev and Nicholas Daniloff, *Grief of My Heart: Memoirs of a Chechen Surgeon* (London: Walker & Company, 2005).

21. Anna Politkovskaya, *A Small Corner of Hell: Dispatches from Chechnya*, trans. Alexander Burry and Tatiana Tulchinsky (Chicago: University of Chicago Press, 2007), Kindle Edition.

22. Ibid., 27.

23. Ibid., 61.

24. Baiev and Daniloff, *Grief of My Heart*, 300.

25. LoCicero and Sinclair, *Creating Young Martyrs*.

26. King James Bible, John 15:13.

27. "President Obama Delivers a Statement on the Passing of Nelson Mandela," The White House, December 5, 2013, http://www.whitehouse.gov/blog/2013/12/05/president-obama-delivers-statement-passing-nelson-mandela.

CHAPTER 3

1. Justin Peters, "Burner Phones, a Scrawled Message on a Boat, and Other Information from the Indictment against Dzhokhar Tsarnaev," *Slate*, June 27, 2013, http://www.slate.com/blogs/crime/2013/06/27/dzhokhar_

tsarnaev_indictment_boston_marathon_bombing_suspect_charged_in
.html. Written in a boat in Watertown, Massachusetts, on April 19, 2013, by Dzhokhar Tsarnaev, awaiting arrest or death.

2. "Boston Marathon Bombings: Suspect Dzhokhar Tsarnaev Left Message in Boat Calling Victims "Collateral Damage," *CBS News*, May 16, 2013, http://www.cbsnews.com/news/boston-marathon-bombings-suspect-dzhokhar-tsarnaev-left-message-in-boat-calling-victims-collateral-damage/. Inexact quote, reportedly written in a boat in a Watertown, Massachusetts, on April 19, 2013, by Dzhokhar Tsarnaev, awaiting arrest or death.

3. Ibid.

4. Reitman, "Jahar's World." Written in a boat in a backyard in Watertown, Massachusetts, on April 19, 2013, by Dzhokhar Tsarnaev, awaiting arrest or death.

5. Martin Daly and Margo Wilson, *Homicide* (New York: Aldine de Gruyer, 1988).

6. King, "Not Your Average Chechen Jihadis."

7. Hays, "In a Brooklyn Courtroom, Terrorists Testify about Subway Suicide Plot." See also Secret, "In Terrorists' Testimony, a Rare, Intimate Look into a Secretive World."

8. Laurence Steinberg, *Youth Violence: Do Parents and Families Make a Difference?* (National Institute of Justice Journal, 2000.)

9. It seems likely that the large number of suicides we see among active-duty and returning American military following deployment in the Afghanistan and Iraq wars may reflect tenuousness of these justifications, leading to more moral engagement than disengagement, resulting in guilt and/or shame.

10. *My Daughter the Terrorist*, directed by Beate Arnestad (The Netherlands: Snit Film Production, 2007), DVD.

11. Fathali Moghaddam, *From the Terrorists' Point of View* (Westport, CT: Praeger, 2006). Moghaddam argues that terrorists are not morally disengaged; it appears that he is equating moral disengagement with lack of morality, rather than using the definition provided by Bandura. Ironically, his work provides good examples of the very processes Bandura describes.

12. Ibid.

13. This sequence captures the essence of Bandura's construct of moral disengagement. The final stage also reflects a concept called "noble cause corruption" by which one acts in a corrupt or immoral way, but considers one's actions to be justified by the importance and virtuousness of the cause. The fallacy here is that the end justifies the means.

14. David C. Pollock and Ruth E. Van Reken, *Third Culture Kids: Growing Up among Worlds*, rev. ed. (Boston: Nicholas Brealey Publishing, 2009), Kindle Edition, 4.

15. Ibid., 90.

16. J. Y., "Chechnya and the Bombs in Boston," The Economist: Eastern Approaches (blog), April 20, 2013, http://www.economist.com/blogs/easternapproaches/2013/04/russian-politics-0.

17. Christa Case Bryant, "Briefing: Palestinian Factions Agree to Reconcile," *Christian Science Monitor*, May 15, 2013, http://www.csmonitor.com/layout/set/r14/World/Middle-East/2013/0515/Briefing-Palestinian-factions-agree-to-reconcile.

18. Shad, *Flying Colours*, Black Box, 2013, liner notes.

19. Ibid.

20. The Telegraph, http://www.telegraph.co.uk/news/worldnews/africaandindianocean/kenya/10573422/Trial-of-Kenya-Westgate-mall-massacre-suspects-opens.html.

21. "My Detainment Story or How I Learned to Stop Feeling Safe in My Own Country and Hate Border Patrol," produced by Sarah Abdurrahman (On The Media, *NPR*, September 20, 2013), http://www.onthemedia.org/story/my-detainment-story-or-how-i-learned-stop-feeling-safe-my-own-country-and-hate-border-patrol/. This report has received considerable attention. On The Media has posted a tool for citizens to use in requesting information from their congressional representatives. Early reports suggest that the information is not easy to come by.

22. Chimamanda Ngozi Adichie, "The danger of a single story," filmed July 2009, TED Video, 18:47, http://www.ted.com/talks/chimamanda_adichie_the_danger_of_a_single_story.html.

23. "Tsarnaevs News Conference: A Transcript," *New York Times*, April 26, 2013, http://www.nytimes.com/2013/04/26/world/europe/tsarnaevs-news-conference-a-transcript.html.

24. Raul Gonzalez, "Performance of Young Adult Cannabis Users on Neurocognitive Measures of Impulsive Behavior and Their Relationship to Symptoms of Cannabis Use Disorders," *Journal of Clinical & Experimental Neuropsychology* 34, no. 9 (2012): 962–76.

25. Moghaddam, *From the Terrorists' Point of View.*

26. Prior to the marathon bombing, Tamerlan was accused of domestic violence, and the boys' mother, Zubeidat, was arrested for shoplifting and destruction of property.

27. "Remembering Stalin's Deportations," *BBC News*, February 23, 2004, http://news.bbc.co.uk/2/hi/3509933.stm. See also "1944–1957:

Deportation and Exile," *The Telegraph*, January 1, 2001, http://www.tele graph.co.uk/news/1399561/1944–1957-Deportation-and-exile.html.

28. Laurence Steinberg and Elizabeth S. Scott, *Rethinking Juvenile Justice.* (Cambridge, MA: Harvard University Press, 2010).

29. Malcolm Gladwell, *Blink* (New York: Little Brown, 2005).

30. "The Teen Brain," *PBS Newshour*, October 13, 2004, http://www .pbs.org/newshour/bb/science/july-dec04/brain_10–13.html.

31. LoCicero and Sinclair, *Creating Young Martyrs*, 41–42.

32. Elias Dakwar, Edward V. Nunes, Adam Bisaga, Kenneth C. Carpenter, John P. Mariani, Maria A. Sullivan, Wilfrid N. Raby, and Francis R. Levin, "A Comparison of Independent Depression and Substance Induced Depression in Cannabis-, Cocaine-, and Opioid-Dependent Treatment Seekers," *American Journal on Addictions* 20, no. 5 (2011): 441–46.

CHAPTER 4

1. Much of this chapter is drawn from an earlier publication by the author. Alice LoCicero, "The Hidden Economics of Promoting Youth Violence," *The New Renaissance* 41 (2010): 18–42. Used by permission of the New Renaissance.

2. The long civil war ended in a successful campaign by the Sri Lankan government in 2009, whose intention was to kill or detain all members of the separatist militia.

3. Quote from a child interviewed by Coalition to End Child Soldiers' staff, southern Sudan, February 2004. *Child Soldiers International*, http://www.child-soldiers.org/childsoldiers/voices-of-young-soldiers.

4. Randall Fegley, "Comparative Perspectives on the Rehabilitation of Ex-Slaves and Former Child Soldiers, with Special Reference to Sudan," *African Studies Quarterly* 10, no. 1 (2008): 35–69, http://www.africa.ufl .edu/asq/v10/v10i1a2.htm, 3.

5. http://www.essex.ac.uk/armedcon/story_id/000215.html.

6. See, for example, Francis Bok, *Escape from Slavery: The True Story of My Ten Years in Captivity and My Journey to Freedom in America* (New York: St Martin's Griffin, 2004). Bok speaks widely on conditions in Sudan, and is affiliated with the American Anti-Slavery Group, found at www.iabolish.org.

7. Robert Barnes, "Supreme Court Restricts Life without Parole for Juveniles," *Washington Post*, May 18, 2010, http://www.washingtonpost .com/wp-dyn/content/article/2010/05/17/AR2010051701355.html.

8. Equal Justice Institute, *Cruel and Unusual: Sentencing 13- and 14-Year Old Children to Die in Prison* (Montgomery, AL: Equal Justice Institute, 2007), 13, www.eji.org.

9. An overview of research on MST, along with reference information, is available on the Internet at http://www.mstservices.com/com plete_overview.php.

10. Lawrence Steinberg and Elizabeth S. Scott, "Less Guilty by Reason of Adolescence: Developmental Immaturity, Diminished Responsibility, and the Juvenile Death Penalty," *American Psychologist* 58 (2003): 1009–1018.

11. From the Harlem Children's Zone (HCZ) website at http://www .hcz.org/about-us/the-hcz-project: "Called 'one of the most ambitious social-service experiments of our time,' by *The New York Times*, the Harlem Children's Zone Project is a unique, holistic approach to rebuilding a community so that its children can stay on track through college and go on to the job market."

12. "Worst forms of child labor" is a phrase used by the International Labor Organization (ILO) to refer specifically to forms of labor with characteristics that place the child at risk. Details are available at the website of the ILO, www.ilo.org.

13. See the Basel Action Network's website, www.ban.org.

14. Ibid.

15. http://www.business-humanrights.org/SpecialRepPortal/Home.

16. Foreword to Jimmie Briggs, *Innocents Lost: When Child Soldiers Go to War* (New York: Basic Books, 2005).

17. Adam Hochschild, "The Trial of Thomas Lubanga," *Atlantic*, December 2009, http://www.theatlantic.com/magazine/archive/2009/12/the-trial-of-thomas-lubanga/307762/.

18. Radhika Coomaraswamy, "Child Soldiers: Root Causes and UN Initiatives," Seminar, Center for the Education of Women, University of Michigan, Ann Arbor, February 2009.

19. Hochschild, "The Trial of Thomas Lubanga."

20. See, for example, Nicholas Kristof, "Striking the Brothels' Bottom Line," *New York Times*, January 11, 2009, http://www.nytimes .com/2009/01/11/opinion/11kristof.html?_r=0.

21. See various columns, such as those noted earlier, and Nicholas Kristof and Sheryl WuDunn, *Half the Sky: Turning Oppression into Opportunity for Women Worldwide* (New York: Knopf, 2009).

22. Kristof and WuDunn, *Half the Sky*, 10.

23. Geoffrey Canada, *Fist, Stick, Knife, Gun* (Boston: Beacon Press, 1995).

See also Marian Wright Edelman's baccalaureate address to Colorado College in 1999, found at http://gos.sbc.edu/e/edelman2.html. In it, she says, "It is adults who manufacture, market, and profit from the guns that have turned many of our neighborhoods and schools into war zones and the blood of children into profit."

24. For more information on this bill, check https://www.govtrack.us /congress/bills/110/s367.

25. See the Basel Action Network's website, www.ban.org.

26. http://www.srsgconsultation.org/index.php/main/discussion? discussion_id=6.

27. Ibid.

28. Those who benefit from drug sales, for example, may immediately buy expensive clothes, shoes, or jewelry. Those who gain even more money may buy mansions or yachts. Thus the money moves rapidly through the alternate economies and back to the mainstream economy. For more information on alternative economies, see Sudhir Alladi Ventakesh, *Off the Books: The Underground Economy of the Urban Poor* (Cambridge, MA: Harvard University Press, 2009).

29. See http://www.hbo.com/the-wire#/the-wire/about/index.html.

30. Michael Wessells, *Child Soldiers: From Violence to Protection* (Cambridge, MA: Harvard University Press, 2006).

31. Marc Pilisuk, *Who Benefits from Global Violence and War* (Westport, CT: Praeger, 2008).

32. Canada, *Fist Stick Knife Gun*, 124

33. Grace Akallo, *Girl Soldier: A Story of Hope for Uganda's Children* (Ada, MI: Baker Publishing Group, 2007), 109.

34. This interviewee was responding to a question about how other countries might help end the war that was then going on in Sri Lanka.

35. Firearms manufactured and advertised exclusively for hunting and shooting game are excluded from consideration here. Although some children are hurt or killed accidentally in using such firearms, the focus here is on firearms intended for use to harm or kill other humans.

36. See Elliot Aronson, Timothy D. Wilson, and Robin M Akert, *Social Psychology*, 7th ed. (Boston: Prentice Hall, 2010). This textbook describes a series of studies consistently demonstrating this principle (see pages 363–64).

37. See for example http://www.crickett.com/index.php?cPath=25.

38. Children's Defense Fund, *State of America's Children 2008 Report*, http://www.childrensdefense.org/child-research-data-publications/data /state-of-americas-children-2008-report.html.

39. "AK-47: The Weapon Changed the Face of War," Hosted by Andrea Seabrook, Weekend Edition Sunday, *NPR*, November 26, 2006, http://www.npr.org/templates/story/story.php?storyId=6539945.

40. M. Kalashnikov, Address to the Participants of the UN Conference on the Illicit Trade in Small Arms and Light Weapons, June 29, 2006, http://www.izhmash.ru/eng/news/300606.shtml.

41. Andrea Seabrook, "AK-47."

42. Mail Foreign Service, "Kalashnikov Awarded Hero of Russia: Lavish Reception for Gunmaker's 90th birthday," *The Daily Mail*, November 10, 2009, http://www.dailymail.co.uk/news/worldnews/article-1226705/Kalashnikov-awarded-Hero-Russia-Lavish-reception-gunmakers-90th-birthday.html.

43. Lowell Bergman, "Gallery of International Arms Dealers," Frontline/World, *PBS*, May 2002, http://www.pbs.org/frontlineworld/stories/sierraleone/breakingnews.html.

44. The Pew Report finds that while one in one hundred Americans is in prison, one in thirty-one American adults are either in prison, on probation, or on parole. See Pew Report "One in 31," http://www.pewstates.org/research/reports/one-in-31-85899371887.

45. See http://www.prisonstudies.org/.

46. http://www.justicereinvestment.org/facts_and_trends.

47. See http://gov.ca.gov/news.php?id=14118.

48. See http://www.apcto.org/.

49. "Prisons for Profit," NOW, *PBS*, May 9, 2008, http://www.pbs.org/now/shows/419/index.html.

50. Ed Pilkington, "Clean Slate for Corrupt Judge's Young Victims in Pennsylvania," *The Guardian*, March 26, 2009, http://www.theguardian.com/world/2009/mar/27/corrupt-judge-pennsylvania-victims.

51. Walter Pavlo, "Pennsylvania Judge Gets 'Life Sentence' for Prison Kickback Scheme," *Forbes*, August 12, 2011, http://www.forbes.com/sites/walterpavlo/2011/08/12/pennsylvania-judge-gets-life-sentence-for-prison-kickback-scheme/.

52. Nicholas Kristof, "If This Isn't Slavery, What Is?" *New York Times*, January 4, 2009, http://www.nytimes.com/2009/01/04/opinion/04kristof.html.

53. Ian Urbina, "For Runaways, Sex Buys Survival," *New York Times*, October 27, 2009, http://www.nytimes.com/2009/10/27/us/27runaways.html?_r=1&sq=prostitution&st=cse&scp=2&pagewanted=print.

54. United Nations Department of Public Information, *Children's Rights*, December 1995, http://www.un.org/rights/dpi1765e.htm.

55. Kristof and WuDunn, *Half the Sky.*, and other work by Nicholas Kristof.

56. Kristof and WuDunn, *Half the Sky*, 10.

CHAPTER 5

1. Clark McCauley, "Jujitsu Politics: Terrorism and Responses," in *Collateral Damage*, ed. Paul R. Kimmel and Chris E. Stout (Westport, CT: Praeger, 2006).

2. This framing, by Zen Buddhist monk and peace activist Thich Nhat Hanh, of the causes of war, violence, and terrorism exists in several places, including an interview with Krista Tippett. See "Transcript for Thich Nhat Hanh on Mindfulness, Suffering, and Engaged Buddhism," produced by Krista Tippett (On Being, *American Public Media*, September 26, 2013), http://www.onbeing.org/program/thich-nhat-hanh-on-mindfulness-suffering-and-engaged-buddhism/transcript/5991.

3. Miriam Wells, "New Ad Campaign Aims to Prevent FARC Child Recruitment," Columbia Reports, November 18, 2011, http://colombiareports.co/colombia-launches-ad-campaign-aimed-at-farc-child-soldiers/.

4. http://rightquestion.org/.

5. Jacobs, Filipov, and Wen, "Fall of the House of Tsarnaev."

6. Estimates are that between 1,000 and 2,000 youth from Western countries, including the United States, are fighting among the rebel forces in the Syrian War at the end of 2013.

7. To see more about these roles, see Moghaddam, *From the Terrorists' Point of View.*

8. Jacobs, Filipov and Wen, "Fall of the House of Tsarnaev."

9. See http://www.publicconversations.org/.

10. Kenneth V. Hardy and Tracey A. Laszloffy, *Teens Who Hurt: Clinical Interventions to Break the Cycle of Adolescent Violence* (New York City: The Guilford Press, 2006).

11. Canada, *Fist, Stick, Knife, Gun.*

12. Elizabeth S. Scott and Laurence Steinberg, *Rethinking Juvenile Justice* (Cambridge, MA: Harvard University Press, 2008).

13. Douglas Stone, Bruce Patton, and Sheila Heen, *Difficult Conversations: How to Discuss What Matters Most* (London: Penguin Books, 1999).

14. Andre Malroux, *Man's Fate*, trans. Haakon Chevalier (New York: Random House, 1961).

15. John Updike, *Terrorist* (New York: Alfred A. Knopf, 2006).

16. Ann Patchett, *Bel Canto* (New York: HarperCollins, 2001).

17. Paul Kimmel and Chris E. Stout, *Collateral Damage* (Westport, CT: Praeger, 2006).

18. "Liberty and Security in a Changing World," *The President's Review Group on Intelligence and Communications Technologies*, December 12, 2013. The text of this report can be found at http://www.theguardian .com/world/interactive/2013/dec/18/nsa-review-panel-report-document.

19. Kristof and WuDunn, *Half the Sky*.

20. John Steinbeck, *Cannery Row* (New York: The Viking Press, 1945).

21. Robert Windrem, "US Government Considered Nelson Mandela a Terrorist until 2008," *NBC News*, December 7, 2013, http://investigations .nbcnews.com/_news/2013/12/07/21794290-us-government-consid ered-nelson-mandela-a-terrorist-until-2008?lite.

22. Juan Manuel Santos, "Why I'm Talking to Terrorists in Colombia," *Wall Street Journal*, September 26, 2013, http://online.wsj.com/news /articles/SB10001424052702303796404579099044159198538.

CHAPTER 6

1. United Nations, "Preamble to the Universal Declaration of Human Rights," 1948, http://www.un.org/en/documents/udhr/.

2. The White House, "Remarks by the President at the Acceptance of the Nobel Peace Prize," December 10, 2009, http://www.whitehouse.gov /the-press-office/remarks-president-acceptance-nobel-peace-prize.

3. Steven Pinker, *The Better Angels of Our Nature: Why Violence Has Declined* (London: Penguin Group, 2011). Kindle Edition. Kindle Locations 10602–3.

4. Agustín Fuentes, *Race, Monogamy, and Other Lies They Told You: Busting Myths about Human Nature* (Berkeley: University of California Press, 2012). Kindle Edition. 118.

5. J. Martin Ramirez, "Moving toward Peace," in *Conflict, Violence, Terrorism, and Their Prevention*, ed. J. M. Ramirez, C. Morrison, and A. J. Kendall (Newcastle upon Tyne, UK: Cambridge Scholars Publishing, 2014).

6. Over time, various groups have initiated news reports that highlight positive events as a counterbalance to the negative news stories. The most successful of these by far is the current news outlet called "Upworthy" (www.upworthy.com) with a readership that has increased to 80 million unique viewers per month in two years. See Ezra Klein, "Does Upworthy Prove Media Outlets Are Hurting Themselves by Publishing So Much Content?" *Washington Post Wonkblog* (blog), December 10, 2013,

http://www.washingtonpost.com/blogs/wonkblog/wp/2013/12/10/does-upworthy-prove-media-outlets-are-hurting-themselves-by-publishing-so-much-content/.

7. The One Percent Doctrine, as described by Ron Suskind in his book of the same name, was based on a statement by Vice-President Dick Cheney, that "if there was even a 1 percent chance of terrorists getting a weapon of mass destruction—and there has been a small probability of such an occurrence for some time—the United States must now act as if it were a certainty." See Ron Suskind, *The One Percent Doctrine* (New York: Simon & Schuster, 2007). This doctrine could be used to support violations of international treaties, including the Geneva Conventions, enhanced interrogation that amounted to torture, extremely high levels of surveillance on American citizens, heavy use of drones, assassinations, sanctions, threats, attacks, wars, profiling, and violations of human rights.

8. In fairness and full disclosure, it is important to acknowledge that the view that violence is not inevitable, that we are not doomed to increasing violence, and that we are not programmed for violence is not universally accepted by biologists or by social scientists. However, this view is gaining acceptance, in part due to a very lucid, well-researched, and well-documented work by Steven Pinker, quoted earlier in the chapter.

9. Cheryl Corley, "Despite the Headlines, Chicago's Crime Rate Fell in 2013," Morning Edition, *NPR*, December 31, 2013, http://www.npr.org/2013/12/31/258413771/despite-the-headlines-chicagos-crime-rate-fell-in-2013.

10. See various sources, including Matt Pearce, "33 Cops Killed by Gunfire in 2013, the Lowest Number since 1887," *Los Angeles Times*, December 30, 2013, http://www.latimes.com/nation/nationnow/la-na-nn-police-deaths-20131230,0,6326138,print.story.

11. D'Vera Cohn, Paul Taylor, Mark Hugo Lopez, Catherine A. Gallagher, Kim Parker, and Kevin T. Maass, "Gun Homicide Rate Down 49% since 1993 Peak; Public Unaware," Pew Research Center Social and Demographic Trends, May 7, 2013. http://www.pewsocialtrends.org/2013/05/07/gun-homicide-rate-down-49-since-1993-peak-public-unaware/.

12. While it seems to many Americans that terrorism is an extraordinary threat to peace, history, reviewed in Chapter 2, reminds us that this is not the first era when terrorism has been perpetrated in the United States, and that terrorism seems to occur intermittently, with each outbreak ending for one of a number of reasons that have been well documented.

13. The White House, "Remarks."

14. Robert H. Jackson, *Opening Statement before the International Military Tribunal*, 1945, http://www.roberthjackson.org/the-man/speeches-articles

/speeches/speeches-by-robert-h-jackson/opening-statement-before-the-international-military-tribunal/.

15. William Schulz, "Despite Setbacks, UN Ushered in 65 Years of Progress on Human Rights," *Christian Science Monitor*, December 10, 2013, http://www.csmonitor.com/Commentary/Opinion/2013/1210/Despite-setbacks-UN-ushered-in-65-years-of-progress-on-human-rights.

16. Pinker, *The Better Angels*.

17. Ibid.

18. United Nations, "Preamble."

19. "About Pugwash," Pugwash website, http://www.pugwash.org/about.htm.

20. "Joseph Rotblat," http://www.nobelprize.org/nobel_prizes/peace/laureates/1995/rotblat-facts.html.

21. Ibid.

22. "The Nobel Peace Prize 1995," Nobelprize.org, http://www.nobelprize.org/nobel_prizes/peace/laureates/1995/.

23. The Russell-Einstein Manifesto of 1955 brought attention to the dangers of nuclear weapons, and advocated for peaceful resolution of conflict. See "Russell-Einstein Manifesto," http://www.pugwash.org/about/manifesto.htm.

24. David S. Greenwald and Steven J. Zeitlin, *No Reason to Talk About It: Families Confront the Nuclear Taboo* (New York: W. W. Norton and Co., 1987). See also Judith Stillion, "Examining the Shadow: Gifted Children Respond to the Threat of Nuclear War," Death Studies 10 (1986): 27–41.

25. Alan Krueger and Jitka Maleckova, "Education, Poverty and Terrorism: Is There a Causal Connection?" *Journal of Economic Perspectives* 17, no. 4 (2003): 119–144.

26. Hardy and Laszloffy, *Teens Who Hurt*.

27. James Gilligan, *Violence: Reflections on a National Epidemic* (New York: Vintage, 1997).

28. Daly and Wilson, *Homicide*, 297.

29. Ibid., 236–37.

30. This finding is consistent with research by Michael Commons and affiliates, revealing that democracy is a social state that is won by steps, and that stateless societies will make a stable movement toward democracy by going through steps in order, rather than skipping steps in order to become a democracy more quickly. See, for example, Michael Commons and Eric Andrew Goodheart, "Consider Stages of Development in Preventing Terrorism: Does Government Building Fail and Terrorism Result When Developmental Stages of Governance Are Skipped?" *Journal of Adult Development* 14 (2007): 91–111.

31. Many sources, including http://plato.stanford.edu/entries/hobbes-moral/.

32. Pinker, *The Better Angels*.

33. While most Americans reject conspiracy theories about 9/11, a surprising number have their doubts. A 2011 CBS News story reported that a poll taken five years after the attack showed that one in three Americans believed that the U.S. government had some role in either causing or allowing the attacks to happen. See Joshua Norman, "9/11 Conspiracy Theories Won't Stop," CBS *News*, September 11, 2011, http://www.cbsnews.com/news/9–11-conspiracy-theories-wont-stop/.

34. Ramirez, "Moving toward Peace."

35. Ibid.

36. The White House, "Remarks."

37. "A Chronology of the IRA Campaign in the 20th Century," *PBS Frontline*, http://www.pbs.org/wgbh/pages/frontline/shows/ira/etc/cron.html.

38. LoCicero and Sinclair, *Creating Young Martyrs*.

39. Jeremy Ginges and Scott Atran, "War as a Moral Imperative (Not Just Practical Politics by Other Means)," *Proceedings of the Royal Society B* 278 (2011): 2930–2938 [Published online February 2011].

40. A very sturdy finding in psychological research is that a common enemy leads otherwise conflicting groups to work together cooperatively. Many accounts and photos from Sri Lanka after the 2004 Indian Ocean tsunami indicate that warring groups lay down their arms and helped one another in the immediate aftermath, only to resume hostilities once the crisis was over. While it would inevitably cause enormous, unpredictable problems, one could imagine that the arrival of some enemy force from another part of the universe, as happens in fiction, would, in reality, bring warring factions of humans into a cooperative arrangement to fight the enemy.

41. Modern scientific pursuits by astrophysicists, such as MacArthur Genius Grant recipient Sara Seager, have recently shown that there are billions of planets that have conditions that could support life forms similar to our own. This very recent announcement has piqued the curiosity of scientists and citizens throughout the world. See Dennis Overbye, "Far Off Planets Like the Earth Dot the Galaxy," *New York Times*, November 4, 2013, http://www.nytimes.com/2013/11/05/science/cosmic-census-finds-billions-of-planets-that-could-be-like-earth.html?_r=0; or Sara Seager, "A Real Search for Alien Life," *TEDxCambridge*, 2013, http://tedxtalks.ted.com/video/A-Real-Search-for-Alien-Life-Sa.

Bibliography

Abdurrahman, Sarah. "My Detainment Story or: How I Learned to Stop Feeling Safe in My Own Country and Hate Border Patrol." On The Media, NPR, September 20, 2013. http://www.onthemedia.org/story/my-detainment-story-or-how-i-learned-stop-feeling-safe-my-own-country-and-hate-border-patrol/.

"About Pugwash," Pugwash website. http://www.pugwash.org/about.htm.

Adichie, Chimamanda Ngozi. "The Danger of a Single Story." Filmed July 2009, TED Video, 18:47. http://www.ted.com/talks/chimamanda_adichie_the_danger_of_a_single_story.html.

Akallo, Grace. Girl Soldier: A Story of Hope for Uganda's Children. Ada, MI: Baker Publishing Group, 2007.

The Applied History Research Group, University of Calgary. "Tamerlane." 2000. http://www.ucalgary.ca/appplied_history/tutor/oldwrld/armies/tamerane.html.

Arizona Military Museum. "Palestinian-Israeli Conflict." http://www.azdema.gov/museum/famousbattles/pdf/Palestinian-Israeli%20Conflict-072809.pdf.

Aronsen, Gavin. "Wrestling Photo, Stunned Reactions from Former Classmates of Bombing Suspect Dzhokhar Tsarnaev." Mother Jones, April 19, 2013. http://www.motherjones.com/print/222656.

Aronson, Elliot, Timothy D. Wilson, and Robin M Akert. Social Psychology, 7th ed. Boston: Prentice Hall, 2010.

Baiev, Khassan, and Nicholas Daniloff. *Grief of My Heart: Memoirs of a Chechen Surgeon*. London: Walker & Company, 2005.

Baiev, Khassan, and Ruth Daniloff. *The Oath: A Surgeon under Fire*. New York: Walker Publishing Company, 2004.

Barnes, Robert. "Supreme Court Restricts Life without Parole for Juveniles." *Washington Post*, May 18, 2010. http://www.washingtonpost .com/wp-dyn/content/article/2010/05/17/AR2010051701355.html.

Barry, Ellen. "Dagestan's Shadow War, Fought by 'Many Tsarnaevs.'" *New York Times*, May 19, 2013. http://www.nytimes.com/2013/05/20/world /europe/bomb-suspects-trip-sheds-light-on-caucasus-war.html?_r=0.

Barry, Ellen. "With Breakdown of Order in Russia's Dagestan Region, Fear Stalks Police." *New York Times*, March 20, 2010. http://www.nytimes .com/2010/03/21/world/europe/21dagestan.html?pagewanted=all.

Bergman, Lowell. "Gallery of International Arms Dealers." Frontline /World, PBS, May 2002. http://www.pbs.org/frontlineworld/stories/sier raleone/breakingnews.html.

Bok, Francis. *Escape from Slavery: The True Story of My Ten Years in Captivity and My Journey to Freedom in America*. New York: St Martin's Griffin, 2004.

"Boston Marathon Bombings: Suspect Dzhokhar Tsarnaev Left Message in Boat Calling Victims "Collateral Damage." *CBS News*, May 16, 2013. http://www.cbsnews.com/news/boston-marathon-bombings-suspect-dz-hokhar-tsarnaev-left-message-in-boat-calling-victims-collateral-damage/.

Briggs, Jimmie. *Innocents Lost: When Child Soldiers Go to War*. New York: Basic Books, 2005.

Brookhiser, Richard. "Domestic Terrorism: The Killers Next Door." *American History* 48, no 4 (2013): 17–18.

Bryant, Christa Case. "Briefing: Palestinian Factions Agree to Reconcile." *Christian Science Monitor*, May 15, 2013. http://www.csmonitor .com/layout/set/r14/World/Middle-East/2013/0515/Briefing-Palestinian-factions-agree-to-reconcile.

Bycowizc, Julie. "Tamerlan Tsarnaev's Family Crumbled before Boston Bombs." *Bloomberg*, April 23, 2013. http://www.bloomberg.com /news/2013-04-23/mom-shoplifts-as-her-boys-become-radicalized.html.

Canada, Geoffrey. *Fist, Stick, Knife, Gun*. Boston: Beacon Press, 1995.

Caryl, Christian. "The Bombers' World." *New York Review of Books*, June 6, 2013. http://www.nybooks.com/articles/archives/2013/jun/06 /bombers-world/.

Cassidy, Chris. "Tsarnaev Family Received $100G in Benefits." *Boston Herald*, April 29, 2013. http://bostonhearlld.com/news_opinion /local_coverage/2013/04/tsarnaev_family_received_100g_in_benefits.

Center for International Development and Conflict Management, University of Maryland. "Chronology of Chechens in Russia." 2010. http://www.cidcm.umd.edu/mar/chronology.asp?groupId=36504.

Children's Defense Fund. State of America's Children 2008 Report. 2008. http://www.childrensdefense.org/child-research-data-publications/data/state-of-americas-children-2008-report.html.

Cohen, Jon. "Most Want Death Penalty for Dzhokhar Tsarnaev if He Is Convicted of Boston Bombing." *Washington Post,* May 1, 2013. http://articles.washingtonpost.com/2013-05-01/world/38940946_1_death-penalty-whites-35-percent.

Commons, Michael, and Eric Andrew Goodheart. "Consider Stages of Development in Preventing Terrorism: Does Government Building Fail and Terrorism Result When Developmental Stages of Governance Are Skipped?" *Journal of Adult Development* 14 (2007): 91–111.

Coomaraswamy, Radhika. "Child Soldiers: Root Causes and UN Initiatives." Seminar, Center for the Education of Women, University of Michigan, Ann Arbor. February 2009.

Corley, Cheryl. "Despite the Headlines, Chicago's Crime Rate Fell in 2013." Morning Edition, *NPR,* December 31, 2013. http://www.npr.org/2013/12/31/258413771/despite-the-headlines-chicagos-crime-rate-fell-in-2013.

Cronin, Audrey Kurth. *How Terrorism Ends.* Princeton, NJ: Princeton University Press, 2009.

Cullison, Alan, Paul Sonne, Anton Troianovski, and David George-Cosh. "Turn to Religion Splits Suspects' Home." *Wall Street Journal,* April 22, 2013. http://online.wsj.com/news/articles/SB100014241278 Cull8732423530457843713125025 9170.

Cullison, Alan, Paul Sonne, and Jennifer Levits. "Life in America Unraveled for Brothers." *Wall Street Journal,* April 20, 2013. http://online.wsj.com/news/articles/SB10001424127887323809304578432501435232278.

Dakwar, Elias, Edward V. Nunes, Adam Bisaga, Kenneth C. Carpenter, John P. Mariani, Maria A. Sullivan, Wilfrid N. Raby, and Francis R. Levin. "A Comparison of Independent Depression and Substance Induced Depression in Cannabis-, Cocaine-, and Opioid-Dependent Treatment Seekers." *American Journal on Addictions* 20, no. 5 (2011): 441–446.

Daly, Martin, and Margo Wilson. *Homicide.* New York: Aldine de Gruyer, 1988.

Dorell, Oren. "Boston Suspects' Mosque Has Ties to Convicted Terrorists, Fugitives and Radical Speakers." *USA Today,* April 23, 2013.

http://www.usatoday.com/story/news/nation/2013/04/23/boston-mosque-radicals/2101411/.

Edelman, Marian Wright. *Baccalaureate Address to Colorado College.* 1999. http://gos.sbc.edu/e/edelman2.html.

Equal Justice Institute. *Cruel and Unusual: Sentencing 13- and 14-Year Old Children to Die in Prison.* Montgomery, AL: Equal Justice Institute, 2007. www.eji.org.

Fegley, Randall. "Comparative Perspectives on the Rehabilitation of Ex-Slaves and Former Child Soldiers, with Special Reference to Sudan." *African Studies Quarterly* 10, no. 1 (2008): 35–69, http://www.africa.ufl.edu/asq/v10/v10i1a2.htm, 3.

Fisher, Marc. "The Tsarnaev Family: A Faded Portrait of an Immigrant's American Dream." *Wall Street Journal*, April 27, 2013. http://www.washingtonpost.com/sf/feature/wp/2013/04/27/the-tsarnaev-family-a-faded-portrait-of-an-immigrants-american-dream/.

Ford, Peter. "Europe Cringes at Bush 'Crusade' against Terrorists." *Christian Science Monitor*, September 19, 2001. http://www.csmonitor.com/2001/0919/p12s2-woeu.html.

Fuentes, Agustin. *Race, Monogamy, and Other Lies They Told You: Busting Myths about Human Nature.* Berkeley: University of California Press, 2012. Kindle edition.

Gilligan, James. *Violence: Reflections on a National Epidemic.* New York: Vintage, 1997.

Ginges, Jeremy, and Scott Atran. "War as a Moral Imperative (Not Just Practical Politics by Other Means)." *Proceedings of the Royal Society B* 278(1720) (2011).

Gonzalez, Raul. "Performance of young Adult Cannabis Users on Neurocognitive Measures of Impulsive Behavior and Their Relationship to Symptoms of Cannabis Use Disorders." *Journal of Clinical & Experimental Neuropsychology* 34, no. 9 (2012): 962–76.

Greenwald, David S., and Steven J. Zeitlin. *No Reason to Talk about It: Families Confront the Nuclear Taboo.* New York: W. W. Norton and Co., 1987.

Hackel, Joyce. "How Does a Boy from a Seaside Town in Norway End Up a Terrorist in Kenya?" The World, *PRI*, October 24, 2013. http://www.pri.org/stories/2013-10-24/how-does-boy-seaside-town-norway-end-terrorist-kenya.

Hardy, Kenneth V., and Tracey A. Laszloffy. *Teens Who Hurt: Clinical Interventions to Break the Cycle of Adolescent Violence.* New York City: The Guilford Press, 2006.

Hays, Tom. "In a Brooklyn Courtroom, Terrorists Testify about Subway Suicide Plot." *Brooklyn Daily Eagle*, April 16, 2012. http://www

.brooklyneagle.com/articles/brooklyn-courtroom-terrorists-testify-about-subway-suicide-plot.

Hester Street. DVD. Directed by Joan Micklin Silver. Midwest Films, 1975.

Hochschild, Adam. "The Trial of Thomas Lubanga." *Atlantic*, December 2009. http://www.theatlantic.com/magazine/archive/2009/12/the-trial-of-thomas-lubanga/307762/.

Hugubakken, Trond. "Norwegian Citizen Possibly Involved in the Terrorist Attack in Kenya." *PST Pressemeldinger*, October 10, 2013. http://www.pst.no/media/pressemeldinger/norwegian-citizen-possibly-involved-in-the-terrorist-attack-in-kenya/.

International Crisis Group. *The North Caucasus: The Challenges of Integration (III), Governance, Elections, Rule of Law*. September 2013 Report. http://www.crisisgroup.org/en/regions/europe/north-caucasus/226-north-caucasus-the-challenges-of-integration-iii-governance-elections-rule-of-law.aspx.

Jackson, Robert H. *Opening Statement before the International Military Tribunal*. 1945. http://www.roberthjackson.org/the-man/speeches-articles/speeches/speeches-by-robert-h-jackson/opening-statement-before-the-international-military-tribunal/.

Jacobs, Sally, David Filipov, and Patricia Wen. "Fall of the House of Tsarnaev." *Boston Globe*, December 15, 2013. http://www.bostonglobe.com/Page/Boston/2011-2020/WebGraphics/Metro/BostonGlobe.com/2013/12/15tsarnaev/tsarnaev.html.

Jewish Virtual Library. "Establishment of Israel." http://www.jewishvirtuallibrary.org/jsource/History/Dec_of_Indep.html.

Jones, Jeffrey M. "U.S. Death Penalty Support Lowest in More Than 40 Years." Gallup, October 29, 2013. http://www.gallup.com/poll/165626/death-penalty-support-lowest-years.aspx.

"Kalashnikov Awarded Hero of Russia: Lavish Reception for Gunmaker's 90th Birthday." *The Daily Mail*, November 10, 2009. http://www.dailymail.co.uk/news/worldnews/article-1226705/Kalashnikov-awarded-Hero-Russia-Lavish-reception-gunmakers-90th-birthday.html.

Kalashnikov, M. Address to the Participants of the UN Conference on the Illicit Trade in Small Arms and Light Weapons. June 29, 2006. http://www.izhmash.ru/eng/news/300606.shtml.

Kimmel, Paul, and Chris E. Stout. *Collateral Damage*. Westport, CT: Praeger, 2006.

King, Charles. "Not Your Average Chechen Jihadis." *Foreign Affairs*, April 21, 2013. http://www.foreignaffairs.com/articles/139333/charles-king/not-your-average-chechen-jihadis.

Klein, Ezra. "Does Upworthy Prove Media Outlets Are Hurting Themselves by Publishing So Much Content?" *Washington Post Wonkblog*

(blog), December 10, 2013. http://www.washingtonpost.com/blogs
/wonkblog/wp/2013/12/10/does-upworthy-prove-media-outlets-are-
hurting-themselves-by-publishing-so-much-content/.

Kotz, Deborah. "Injury Toll from Marathon Bombs Reduced to 264."
Boston Globe, April 24, 2013. http://www.bostonglobe.com/lifestyle
/health-wellness/2013/04/23/number-injured-marathon-bombing-
revised-downward/NRpaz5mmvGquP7KMA6XsIK/story.html.

Kovalyova, Albina, and Alastair Jamieson. "Female Suicide Bomber
Suspected of Russia Bus Blast: At Least Five Dead." *NBC News*,
October 21, 2013. http://worldnews.nbcnews.com/_news/2013/10/21
/21062945-female-suicide-bomber-suspected-of-russia-bus-blast-
at-least-5-dead?lite.

Kristof, Nicholas. "If This Isn't Slavery, What Is?" *New York Times*, January 4, 2009. http://www.nytimes.com/2009/01/04/opinion/04kristof
.html.

Kristof, Nicholas. "Striking the Brothels' Bottom Line." *New York Times*,
January 11, 2009. http://www.nytimes.com/2009/01/11/opinion/11kris
tof.html?_r=0.

Kristof, Nicholas, and Sheryl WuDunn. *Half the Sky: Turning Oppression
into Opportunity for Women Worldwide*. New York: Knopf, 2009.

Krueger, Alan, and Jitka Maleckova. "Education, Poverty and Terrorism:
Is There a Causal Connection?" *Journal of Economic Perspectives* 17,
no. 4 (2003): 119–44.

Libell, Henrik Pryser, and Nicholas Kulish. "In Kenya Inquiry, Norway
Looks at Somali Migrant." *New York Times*, October 18, 2013. http://
www.nytimes.com/2013/10/19/world/africa/norway-suspect-nairobi-
kenya-mall-siege.html.

LoCicero, Alice. "The Hidden Economics of Promoting Youth Violence."
The New Renaissance 41 (2010): 18–42.

LoCicero, Alice, and Samuel J. Sinclair. *Creating Young Martyrs: Conditions That Make Dying in a Terrorist Attack Seem Like a Good Idea*.
Westport, CT: Praeger, 2008.

LoCicero, Alice, and Samuel J. Sinclair. "Terrorism and Terrorist Leaders: Insights from Developmental and Ecological Psychology." *Studies
in Conflict and Terrorism* 31, no. 3 (2008): 227–50.

Malroux, Andre. *Man's Fate*. Translated by Haakon Chevalier. New York:
Random House, 1961.

McCauley, Clark. "Jujitsu Politics: Terrorism and Responses." In *Collateral
Damage*, edited by Paul R. Kimmel and Chris E. Stout. Westport, CT:
Praeger, 2006.

Moghaddam, Fathali. *From the Terrorists' Point of View*. Westport, CT: Praeger, 2006.

Murphy, Kim, Joseph Tanfani, and Sergei L. Loiko. "The Tsarnaev Brothers' Troubled Trail to Boston." *Los Angeles Times*, April 28, 2013. http://www.latimes.com/news/nationworld/nation/la-na-boston-suspects-20130428-dto,0,15030.htmlstory#axzz2l1NGQoaH.

My Daughter the Terrorist. DVD. Directed by Beate Arnestad. The Netherlands: Snit Film Production, 2007.

Myers, Steven Lee. "Bombings Jolt Russia, Raising Olympic Fears." *New York Times*, December 30, 2013. http://www.nytimes.com/2013/12/30/world/europe/volgograd-russia-explosion.html?hpw&rref=world.

"1944–1957: Deportation and Exile." *The Telegraph*, January 1, 2001. http://www.telegraph.co.uk/news/1399561/1944-1957-Deportation-and-exile.html.

"The Nobel Peace Prize 1995." Nobelprize.org. http://www.nobelprize.org/nobel_prizes/peace/laureates/1995/.

Norman, Joshua. "9/11 Conspiracy Theories Won't Stop." *CBS News*, September 11, 2011. http://www.cbsnews.com/news/9-11-conspiracy-theories-wont-stop/.

"Norway Tried to Stop Hassan Abdi Dhuhulow, One of Westgate Mall Attackers." *Epoch Times*, October 23, 2013. http://www.theepochtimes.com/n3/327184-norway-tried-to-stop-hassan-abdi-dhuhulow-one-of-westgate-mall-attackers/.

Ohlheiser, Abby. "Most Boston Residents Wouldn't Give Dzhokhar Tsarnaev the Death Penalty." *The Atlantic Wire*, September 16, 2013. http://www.theatlanticwire.com/national/2013/09/boston-residents-wouldnt-give-dzhokhar-tsarnaev-death-penalty/69468/.

Ortiz, Eric. "'He Was Just Relaxed': After Attack, Boston Marathon Bombing Suspect Dzhokhar Tsarnaev Partied, Went to Gym." *New York Daily News*, April 20, 2013. http://www.nydailynews.com/news/crime/dzhokhar-tsarnaev-partied-gym-days-bombing-article-1.1322828.

Parfitt, Tom. "Boston Bombers' Father to Travel to US to Bury Tamerlan Tsarnaev." *The Telegraph*, April 25, 2013. http://www.telegraph.co.uk/news/worldnews/northamerica/usa/10019201/Boston-bombers-father-to-travel-to-US-to-bury-Tamerlan-Tsarnaev.html.

Patchett, Ann. *Bel Canto*. New York: HarperCollins, 2001.

Paterson, Tony. "Neo-Nazi Nuremberg: Germany Forced to Confront Its Dark Side." *The Independent*, May 3, 2013. http://www.independent.co.uk/news/world/europe/neonazi-nuremberg-germany-forced-to-confront-its-dark-side-8602738.html.

Pavlo, Walter. "Pennsylvania Judge Gets 'Life Sentence' for Prison Kickback Scheme." *Forbes*, August 12, 2011. http://www.forbes.com /sites/walterpavlo/2011/08/12/pennsylvania-judge-gets-life-sentence-for-prison-kickback-scheme/.

PBS Frontline. "A Chronology of the IRA Campaign in the 20th Century." http://www.pbs.org/wgbh/pages/frontline/shows/ira/etc/cron.html.

Pearce, Matt. "33 Cops Killed by Gunfire in 2013, the Lowest Number since 1887." *Los Angeles Times*, December 30, 2013. http://www.latimes.com /nation/nationnow/la-na-nn-police-deaths-20131230,0,6326138,print .story.

Peters, Justin. "Burner Phones, a Scrawled Message on a Boat, and Other Information from the Indictment against Dzhokhar Tsarnaev." *Slate*, June 27, 2013. http://www.slate.com/blogs/crime/2013/06/27/dzhokhar_ tsarnaev_indictment_boston_marathon_bombing_suspect_charged_ in.html.

Pew Research Center. "One in 31." March 2, 2009. http://www.pewstates .org/research/reports/one-in-31-85899371887.

Pilisuk, Marc. *Who Benefits from Global Violence and War*. Westport, CT: Praeger, 2008.

Pilkington, Ed. "Clean Slate for Corrupt Judge's Young Victims in Pennsylvania." *The Guardian*, March 26, 2009. http://www.theguardian .com/world/2009/mar/27/corrupt-judge-pennsylvania-victims.

Pinker, Steven. *The Better Angels of Our Nature: Why Violence Has Declined*. London: Penguin Group, 2011. Kindle edition.

Politkovskaya, Anna. *A Small Corner of Hell: Dispatches from Chechnya*. Translated by Alexander Burry and Tatiana Tulchinsky. Chicago: University of Chicago Press, 2007. Kindle edition.

Pollock, David C., and Ruth E. Van Reken. *Third Culture Kids: Growing Up among Worlds*, Rev. Ed. Boston: Nicholas Brealey Publishing, 2009. Kindle edition.

"Pope Francis' Letter to Grand Imam of Al-Azhar Calls for Mutual Understanding between Christians And Muslims." *Huffington Post*, September 18, 2013. http://www.huffingtonpost.com/2013/09/18/pope-francis-letter-al-azhar_n_3948461.html.

The President's Review Group on Intelligence and Communications Technologies. "Liberty and Security in a Changing World." December 12, 2013.

"Prisons for Profit." NOW, PBS, May 9, 2008. http://www.pbs.org/now /shows/419/index.html.

Radia, Kirit. "Bomb Suspects' Mother Says Young Son Would Have Obeyed Older Brother." Good Morning America, ABC News, April 22, 2013. http://abcnews.go.com/International/boston-bomb-suspects-mother-young-son-obeyed-big/story?id=19014490.

Ramirez, J. Martin. "Moving toward Peace." In *Conflict, Violence, Terrorism, and Their Prevention*, edited by J. M. Ramirez, C. Morrison, and A. J. Kendall. Newcastle upon Tyne, UK: Cambridge Scholars Publishing, 2014.

Reitman, Janet. "Jahar's World." *Rolling Stone*, August 1, 2013. http://www.rollingstone.com/culture/news/jahars-world-20130717.

"Remembering Stalin's deportations." *BBC News*, February 23, 2004. http://news.bbc.co.uk/2/hi/3509933.stm.

Richardson, Louise. *What Terrorists Want: Understanding the Enemy, Containing the Threat*. New York: Random House, 2007.

Riley-Smith, Jonathan. *The Crusades, Christianity, and Islam (Bampton Lectures in America)*. New York: Columbia University Press, 2008. Kindle edition.

Rocca, Francis X. "Muslim Seminary Ends Talks with Vatican over Pope's Comments." *Huffington Post*, January 20, 2011. http://www.huffington post.com/2011/01/20/muslim-seminary-ends-talk_n_811839.html.

Rotella, Sebastian. "Boston Bombing Suspects Echo Home-Grown Terrorists in Madrid, London Attacks." *Propublica*, April 20, 2013. http://www.propublica.org/article/boston-bombing-suspects-echo-home-grown-terrorists-in-madrid-london-att.

Saltzman, Amy. "Slain Bombing Suspect Had Arrest Record in Cambridge." *Wicked Local Cambridge*, April 20, 2013. http://www.wicked local.com/cambridge/news/x1148865564/Slain-bombing-suspect-had-arrest-record-in-Cambridge#.

Santos, Juan Manuel. "Why I'm Talking to Terrorists in Colombia." *Wall Street Journal*, September 26, 2013. http://online.wsj.com/news/articles /SB10001424052702303796404579099044159198538.

Schulz, William. "Despite Setbacks, UN Ushered in 65 Years of Progress on Human Rights." *Christian Science Monitor*, December 10, 2013. http://www.csmonitor.com/Commentary/Opinion/2013/1210/Despite-setbacks-UN-ushered-in-65-years-of-progress-on-human-rights.

Scott, Elizabeth S., and Laurence Steinberg. *Rethinking Juvenile Justice*. Cambridge: Harvard University Press, 2008.

Seabrook, Andrea. "AK-47: The Weapon Changed the Face of War." Weekend Edition Sunday, *NPR*, November 26, 2006. http://www.npr .org/templates/story/story.php?storyId=6539945.

Secret, Mosi. "In Terrorists' Testimony, a Rare, Intimate Look into a Secretive World." *New York Times*, April 29, 2012. http://www .nytimes.com/2012/04/30/nyregion/testimony-of-4-admitted-terrorists-gives-a-rare-view-of-al-qaeda.html?_r=0.

"Seven Year Anniversary of the Murder of Anna Politkovskaya." *U.S. Department of State Press Statement*, October 7, 2013. http://www.state .gov/r/pa/prs/ps/2013/10/215185.htm.

Sontag, Deborah, David Herszenhorn, and Serge F. Kovaleski. "A Battered Dream, Then a Violent Path." *New York Times*, April 27, 2013. http://www.nytimes.com/2013/04/28/us/shot-at-boxing-title-denied-tamerlan-tsarnaev-reeled.html?_r=0.

Steinbeck, John. *Cannery Row*. New York: The Viking Press, 1945.

Steinberg, Lawrence, and Elizabeth S. Scott. "Less Guilty by Reason of Adolescence: Developmental Immaturity, Diminished Responsibility, and the Juvenile Death Penalty." *American Psychologist* 58 (2003): 1009–1018.

Steinberg, Lawrence, and Elizabeth S. Scott. *Rethinking Juvenile Justice*. Cambridge, MA: Harvard University Press, 2010.

Stillion, Judith. "Examining the Shadow: Gifted Children Respond to the Threat of Nuclear War." *Death Studies* 10 (1986): 119–44.

Stone, Douglas, Bruce Patton, and Sheila Heen. *Difficult Conversations: How to Discuss What Matters Most*. London: Penguin Books, 1999.

Suskind, Ron. *The One Percent Doctrine*. New York: Simon and Schuster, 2007.

Swaine, Jon. "Tamerlan Tsarnaev's Wife Katherine Russell Wore the Hijab after Converting to Islam." *The Telegraph*, April 20, 2013. http://www.telegraph.co.uk/news/worldnews/northamerica/usa/10007326/Tamerlan-Tsarnaevs-wife-Katherine-Russell-wore-the-hijab-after-converting-to-Islam.html.

"Timeline: A Look at Tamerlan Tsarnaev's Past." *CNN*, April 22, 2013. http://www.cnn.com/2013/04/21/us/tamerlan-tsarnaev-timeline/.

Tippett, Krista. "Transcript for Thich Nhat Hanh on Mindfulness, Suffering, and Engaged Buddhism." On Being, *American Public Media*, September 26, 2013. http://www.onbeing.org/program/thich-nhat-hanh-on-mindfulness-suffering-and-engaged-buddhism/transcript/5991.

"Tsarnaevs News Conference: A Transcript." *New York Times*, April 26, 2013. http://www.nytimes.com/2013/04/26/world/europe/tsarnaevs-news-conference-a-transcript.html.

United Nations. "Preamble to the Universal Declaration of Human Rights." 1948. http://www.un.org/en/documents/udhr/.

Updike, John. *Terrorist*. New York: Alfred A. Knopf, 2006.

Urbina, Ian. "For Runaways, Sex Buys Survival." *New York Times*, October 27, 2009. http://www.nytimes.com/2009/10/27/us/27runaways.html?_r=1&sq=prostitution&st=cse&scp=2&pagewanted=print.

Ventakesh, Sudhir Alladi. *Off the Books: The Underground Economy of the Urban Poor*. Cambridge, MA: Harvard University Press, 2009.

Wells, Miriam. "New Ad Campaign Aims to Prevent FARC Child Recruitment." *Colombia Reports*, November 18, 2011. http://colombiareports.co/colombia-launches-ad-campaign-aimed-at-farc-child-soldiers/.

Wessells, Michael. *Child Soldiers: From Violence to Protection.* Cambridge, MA: Harvard University Press, 2006.

The White House. "President Obama Delivers a Statement on the Passing of Nelson Mandela." December 5, 2013. http://www.whitehouse.gov/blog/2013/12/05/president-obama-delivers-statement-passing-nelson-mandela.

The White House. "Remarks by the President at the Acceptance of the Nobel Peace Prize." December 10, 2009. http://www.whitehouse.gov/the-press-office/remarks-president-acceptance-nobel-peace-prize.

The White House. "Statement by the President." April 19, 2013. http://www.whitehouse.gov/the-press-office/2013/04/19/statement-president.

Windrem, Robert. "US Government Considered Nelson Mandela a Terrorist until 2008." *NBC News*, December 7, 2013. http://investigations.nbcnews.com/_news/2013/12/07/21794290-us-government-considered-nelson-mandela-a-terrorist-until-2008?lite.

Wines, Michael, and Ian Lovett. "The Dark Side, Carefully Masked." *New York Times*, May 4, 2013. http://www.nytimes.com/2013/05/05/us/dzhokhar-tsarnaevs-dark-side-carefully-masked.html.

Y., J. "Chechnya and the bombs in Boston." *The Economist: Eastern Approaches* (blog), April 20, 2013. http://www.economist.com/blogs/easternapproaches/2013/04/russian-politics-0.

Index

About the Author

Alice LoCicero, PhD, is a clinical and research psychologist who lives in Cambridge, Massachusetts. She is a core faculty member at the Center for Multicultural Training in Psychology at Boston Medical Center and an adjunct faculty member at Lesley University. LoCicero has focused her research on children recruited to lives immersed in violence around the world. She has met with numerous youth victims of trauma from five continents. She is co-founder and past president of the Society for Terrorism Research. In 2007 and 2010, Dr. LoCicero traveled to Sri Lanka, where she interviewed children affected by the Indian Ocean tsunami, civil war, and terrorism. She reported on her early work in Sri Lanka in the book *Creating Young Martyrs: Conditions That Make Dying in a Terrorist Attack Seem Like a Good Idea.* In earlier parts of her career, Dr. LoCicero was a staff psychologist at Children's Hospital, Boston, and a faculty member at Tufts University and at Harvard Medical School.